GARDENS
by the Sea

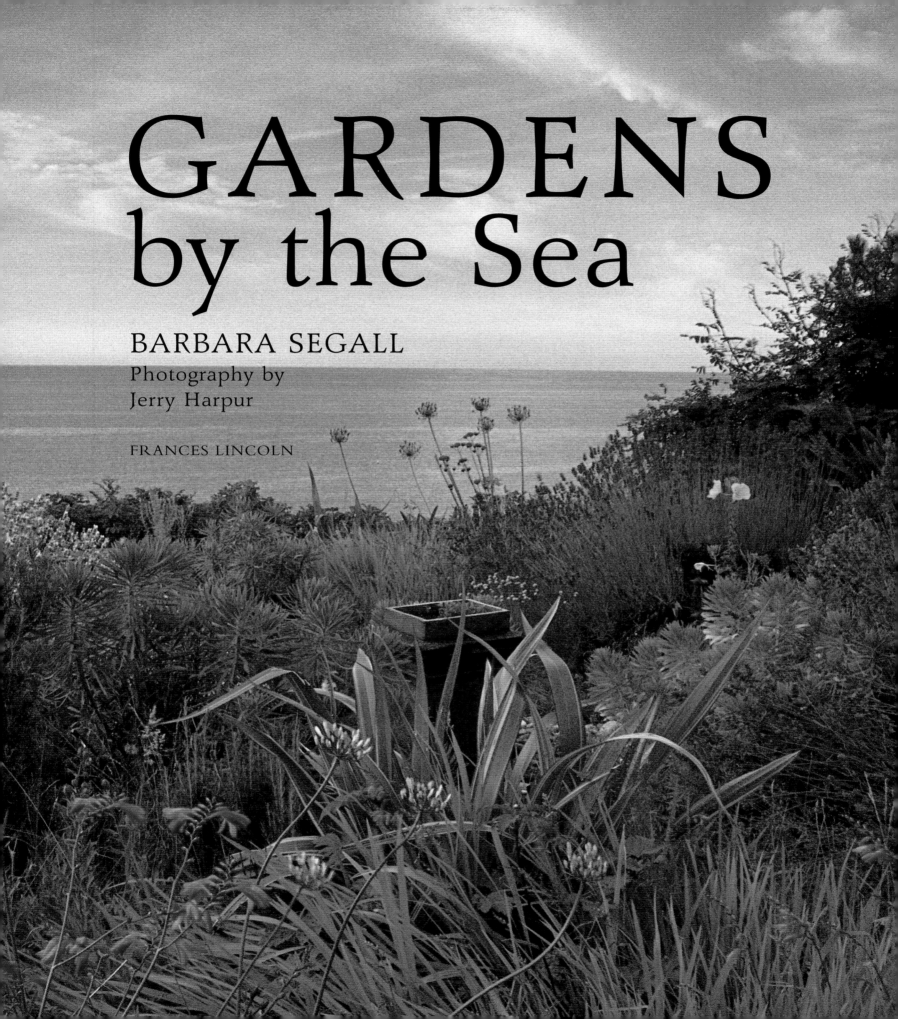

GARDENS
by the Sea

BARBARA SEGALL

Photography by
Jerry Harpur

FRANCES LINCOLN

For my parents, Ada and Freemie Segall

Frances Lincoln Limited
4 Torriano Mews
Torriano Avenue
London NW5 2RZ
www.franceslincoln.com

Gardens by the Sea
Copyright © Frances Lincoln Limited 2002
Original text copyright © Barbara Segall 2002
Photographs copyright © Jerry Harpur 2002 except for those
on pages 94–9, 130 (top) and 131
copyright © Steven Wooster 2002

First Frances Lincoln edition: 2002

British Library Cataloguing-in-Publication Data
A catalogue record for this book is available from the
British Library.

ISBN 0 7112 1894 3

Set in ATWile

Printed and bound in Singapore

2 4 6 8 9 7 5 3 1

TITLE PAGE The combination of low-growing, mounded shrubs and perennials at
Highover, Devon, stands up well to winds off the sea and allow for uninterrupted views
across the ocean. Narrow gravelled paths wind through the plants, leading to a circular
gravelled area where you can sit down, relax and take in the view.

ABOVE In some coastal gardens the view across the water dominates; in others it may
be obscured by plants. Here in the island garden of Villa San Michele, Capri, a stone
sphinx gazes out to sea from one of many vantage points.

RIGHT Agaves of varying shapes and degree of spiny foliage float above a carpet of
colourful sedums at Carol Valentine's Santa Barbara, California, garden, designed by
Isobel Greene & Associates.

CONTENTS

INTRODUCTION

There are hundreds of thousands of miles of coastline around the globe. Not all are populated, but there are clear commercial and mercantile reasons why centres of population have arisen near marine ports at sites around the coastal areas of every country in the world. Settlements have always grown up near ports, and for centuries people have travelled to coastal towns and resorts to take advantage of the health-giving benefits of the sea air and salt water.

I grew up in a seaside resort, on the north coast of South Africa's Natal province on the Indian Ocean. The basic population swelled in the holiday season when the upcountry folk rushed down to the sea for a week or two. But for those of us who lived there all year round, the sea was a constant feature of daily life.

Walls draped with bougainvillea and pink clouds of Honolulu creeper (*Antigonon leptopus*), hedges of acalypha and fiery crotons are among the seaside garden flowers of my childhood home. At the lawn's edge low retaining walls filled with purple mesembryanthemums and containers of spiky aloes formed the boundary between garden, sea and sky. Here the garden was on a sandbank some 60 metres/200 feet above the rocky shore where I spent every afternoon. Barnacle-encrusted rocks, clear rock pools, splashed and refreshed with every tide and filled with exotic sea creatures, were my playground. Later I grew to enjoy walking along the scalloped tide marks, eyes down, looking for cuttlefish, shells and pebbles, sea-washed glass and pieces of seaweed and driftwood.

At that time, although I appreciated how beautiful my mother's garden was, I was unaware of the challenges that she met in creating this flower-filled enclosure. Now I understand how much the garden benefited from the shelter belts she planted, and how it was based on a careful choice of plants that were native or else exotics that enjoyed similar conditions in their country of origin. I know now that the grass was always green because it was a tough, rather invasive species that survived on and stabilized the light, sandy soil of the garden. The garden was a haven for bird and insect life, attracted by the nectar-rich flowers that bloomed through the summer. Bright yellow weaver birds used the grass and she-oak (*Allocasuarina littoralis*) foliage to practise their knot-making skills and weave their funnel-shaped basket nests into the indigenous trees in the garden's walled courtyard.

Although this, my first and only day-to-day experience of seaside gardening, is way back in my childhood, in a sunlit, sky-blue world, the sea is always there in my mind and I suppose it is the pull of the tide that has drawn me towards these special places. When you live at the seaside, you become captivated by change. Those who come on holiday enjoy it – they hope – in its holiday mood, but if you are a resident you are aware of the constant changes in light, in the

The purity of the light, the changing moods of the sea and the sky, and the freshness of the air are among the advantages of living by the sea. And there is drama too.

ABOVE In the Hanauers' garden in Long Island it made sense to position the deck in the best place to sit and enjoy the view. The deck is connected to the house by means of a timber walkway. Shade is provided by wind-shaped choke cherry trees (*Prunus virginiana*).

RIGHT When Naila and Ian Green came to Highover, Devon, there was a fence at the cliff edge. Straightaway they removed it so that they could enjoy the dramatic view, with the sea as the fourth dimension of their garden, both backdrop and leading player. Now the shrubby *Rosa* 'Fru Dagmar Hastrup', which suckers freely, grows well at the cliff edge. It marks the boundary and prevents visitors going too close to the edge. It also provides a first line of shelter, filtering wind off the coast, and its suckering growth habit helps to stabilize the cliff edge.

shape of the waves, of the mood of the sea, of the play of the wind. Whether your garden is low down on the shoreline, near dunes and beaches, or on coastal cliffs, or even a little inland from the shore, you find that the sea is the fourth dimension.

The ever-present sea is the most majestic of backdrops. It can also sometimes come a little too close for comfort – most dramatically at times of storm, when it can inundate gardens, sweeping away plants and mulches. On a more mundane level, seaside soil is often thin and poor, with low nutrient levels, and plants often have to suffer the assaults of drying or salt-laden winds.

Don't be misled, however, into believing that seaside conditions, or indeed seaside style, can only exist at the coast. Some inland gardeners are closet seaside gardeners. There are those, like me, who are seaside gardeners *manqué*. Our gardens are not challenged by the damaging effects of salt burn or sea inundation, but many are on exposed sites where drying winds are as deleterious. Many rooftop gardeners find themselves gardening in a situation not unlike that of a clifftop garden. So many of the techniques that seaside gardeners employ are just as useful for success with exposed inland gardens. There are also those who would like to garden by the seaside and, as the next best thing, create gardens inland using a range of plants and beach paraphernalia to conjure up a seaside atmosphere.

In *Gardens by the Sea* photographer Jerry Harpur and I have assembled a collection of some twenty-one gardens in England, Scotland, the Mediterranean, Scandinavia, the United States of America, New Zealand and Australia. These gardens are all within sight of the sea and, for their owners, the sea is as much part of the garden as is the grass or the border. Its influence is felt in the choice of plants and the style of the garden: the gardens all involve inspired plant choices that are right for the site and its limitations. Some of these gardens may seem almost too good to be true, the dream gardens of the coast. But there is no reason why you should not take hold of these seaside dreams and make them, or elements of them, work in your own garden.

In the plants section I have listed most of the signature plants of these gardens, plus others that are the bread and butter of seaside gardens in different climates. Coastal gardeners have been compiling lists of plants that do and don't do at the seaside at least since *Seaside Planting of Trees and Shrubs* by A. Gaut was published in 1907. Today coastal gardeners and writers are expanding their own lists, as they try out new species and varieties.

At any frontier there is always a little lawlessness, and at the seaside this often takes the shape of whimsy. Beachcombing is a way of life for those who live near the sea. A twist of driftwood, a collection of shells or water-rubbed glass, netting, rope: all are grist to the mill of the seaside artist and are likely to appear as finishing touches to the drama that is seaside gardening.

GARDENS BY THE SEA

A SHELTERED GARDEN

CORNWALL, ENGLAND

The garden at Lamorran House in southwest Cornwall overlooks the sheltered Fal estuary. Where the site slopes down to the south, to the bay, it is protected by the small headland of St Anthony, which blocks most of the southwest wind. On the other three sides the garden is open to the sea and therefore to the potentially damaging influences of fierce salt-laden winds off the Atlantic. When the present owners, Mr and Mrs Robert Dudley-Cooke, moved here in 1982 their priority was to mitigate the winds' effects by planting sheltering trees and establishing well-sited enclosed planting areas.

With the wind factor in check, the garden's proximity to the warming Gulf Stream has created a benign microclimate which allows the Dudley-Cookes to grow a variety of rare palm trees and tender plants. Warm air held in the bay below rises through the garden. Easterly winds are now blocked by the shelter belts and the north winds blow over the top. Severe, lasting frosts are rare in this favoured site, with the most recent recorded in 1987 (-8°C/18°F for two consecutive nights) and 1997 (-3°C/27°F for one night only). However, although tender evergreens do well at Lamorran, the Cornish climate is not hot enough to provide semi-tropical climbers, such as bougainvillea, with the summer-long baking that they need.

The 1.6 hectare/4 acre garden has been in the making over the two decades since the Dudley-Cookes bought the property. At that time near the house was a relatively flat area planted with herbaceous plants. Below, much more steeply sloping, was a tangle of blackthorn and bramble and, at sea level, a copse of self-sown hawthorn, all of which had to be cleared.

The garden at Lamorran House descends through several terraces to the sea, by means of winding paths, viewpoints and intimate, plant-filled compartments. Shelter belts of trees and the protection offered by enclosed garden rooms allow Mediterranean and sub-tropical plants to thrive.

LEFT The Chusan palm (*Trachycarpus fortunei*), which is reliably hardy in Britain, is a signature plant within the garden. It is used in short avenues as well as combined with other palms including Canary Island palms and the jelly palm (*Butia capitata*). Arctotis and gazanias colour the understorey beneath the palms.

FAR LEFT The lower and most recently planted area of the garden has a distinctly Mediterranean atmosphere. Statuary and architectural features, such as these columns that frame the view, combine with plants such as agave and Chusan palm to add to this impression.

Although flowering shrubs and perennials, including rhododendrons, provide seasonal colour, foliage plays a key role in the garden's overall look. Here shapely banana leaves vie with the spiky shapes of cordylines, agaves and palms, each providing drama, texture and shape.

On the eastern side were a few good trees – *Chamaecyparis lawsoniana, Cupressus macrocarpa* 'Goldcrest', two Monterey pines (*Pinus radiata*), and an Austrian pine – which still survive. Overgrown specimens of *Olearia traversii* and *O. macrodonta* were removed and replaced with more Monterey pines and twenty different eucalypts, planted in copses to form sheltering groups. To the north of the house, on the skyline where it did catch the wind, was a row of Monterey pines eighty to ninety years old: its survival indicated that Monterey pines would be a good choice for the new shelter belt, and so they have proved.

The house is on the highest part of the site. From it paths wind down to sea level, leading to numerous small, intimate and plant-enclosed compartments, many with pools, and all with warm-temperate and sub-tropical planting. Arches, balustrades, statues, a ruined temple, steps and retaining walls in Cornish stone all add to the visual interest and a distinctly Japanese feel manifests itself in the shape of stone lanterns, granite boulders and grey gravel.

The Dudley-Cookes' first planting was of rhododendrons and azaleas that they brought from their previous garden in Surrey. Very soon, however, Robert Dudley-Cooke realized that this site could accommodate much rarer and more tender plants and the garden became more and more Mediterranean in atmosphere. The soil – an acid, sandy loam, fertile yet well drained – helps ensure the establishment and health of layer upon layer of architecturally dramatic plants. Dividing the garden into small compartments created very sheltered areas and allowed many tender plants to be grown, including a wide range of palm trees, spiky aloes, agaves, cordylines and puyas, and large numbers of the Australian tree fern (*Dicksonia antarctica*). Among them the azaleas and rhododendrons still thrive, now joined by ceanothus and cistus. The over-arching effect is of a Riviera-like luxuriance, disclosing at each and every turn a tantalizing, foliage-framed view through to the yacht-studded estuary.

Palms, so reminiscent of Mediterranean shorelines, are a major feature in the garden, with Lamorran credited as the most northerly palm garden in the world. Providing the temperatures are favourable, the leathery leaflets of many palms withstand wind well, yielding to and filtering its worst effects. The jelly palm (*Butia capitata*) has arched feather-shaped leaves. *B. yatay*, another shapely South American palm, has survived some particularly cold weather when the *Trachycarpus fortunei*, thought to be much hardier, suffered from leaf scorch. The Canary Island date palm (*Phoenix canariensis*), one of which is now 6 metres/20 feet high and with a similar spread, the European fan palm (*Chamaerops humilis*), and *C.h.* var. *argentea* have been joined by new plantings of an American fan palm (*Sabal bermudana*), the majestic queen palm (*Syagrus romanzoffiana,* syn. *Arecastrum romanzoffianum*) and the desert fan palm (*Washingtonia filifera*).

On the house terrace, pots of citrus trees revel in the warmth, while against the wall there flourishes the rarely seen *Sesbania punicea*, a leguminous shrub with vermilion pea flowers generally recommended for a stove house.

At the bottom of the garden, a pretty Venetian-style bridge over a stream allows an uninterrupted view of the sea. The ground falls away below the bridge, revealing a rock face planted with orange gazanias and a rich yellow arctotis (*Arctotis* × *hybrida* 'Apricot'). The intriguing elephant's foot (*Nolina recurvata*), a member of the agave family, grows here with dasylirions and bear grass and opuntias, all thriving in the stony soil and the mild maritime climate.

Several plants have seeded themselves throughout the garden. *Luma apiculata* (syn. *Myrtus luma*) with small dark green leaves, fine cinnamon-coloured bark and white flowers in late summer and autumn, has almost become a weed. *Echium pininana* seeds prolifically too. It is allowed to stay if the position is good, and produce its massive spike of blue flowers which can reach 4 metres/13 feet high. Several echiums are good coastal plants and this particular variety will survive a degree or two of frost.

As the plants grow, they mass together, creating even more shelter. You cannot see the soil even in winter, for virtually all the plants are evergreens. There is continuous growth and what lawns there are, near the house, have to be cut all year round.

ABOVE LEFT Chusan palms line the stone steps that lead to the small semi-circular pool. Plants and architectural features including this well-sited archway help to protect and shelter plants, as well as frame and disclose dramatic views.

ABOVE RIGHT Although the overall atmosphere is of a Mediterranean or Riviera garden, each little secret or compartment garden has its own character. Here a Japanese style, suggested by stone lanterns, gravel and boulders, blends with more classical structures.

SEASIDE TERRACES

CAPRI, ITALY

On some coastal gardens the mantle of potential seaside vicissitudes sits lightly. At the hillside terraced garden of Villa Anacapri, on the island of Capri, many of the problems found in other seaside gardens are absent.

Although the ground is essentially stony the soil on the terraces is good, because it has been cultivated for centuries, with topsoil being imported by successive gardeners and owners to ameliorate the original soil. The garden is exposed to winds from the north and northwest but, luckily, these are mostly confined to winter. The garden suffers from summer heat and drought, and plants in containers need special watering regimes, but most of the plants on the terraces are well adapted to drought conditions. The lawn of the terrace, the Prato Rustico, is planted with drought-resistant grass. The other lawns are planted with *Zoysia* species, low maritime grasses, useful for warm climates.

From Villa Anacapri, perched atop its terraced garden, there are views to the island of Ischia and across the Mediterranean to the even smaller island of Procida, and down below to the small bays of the beautiful rocky coastline. The house is a white stuccoed Mediterranean villa, and, typically, is built on the upper part of the site, with the garden descending via terraces towards the sea. The terraces are ancient, supported on stone retaining walls built by previous owners, and originally created to grow olives and grapes.

This part of Capri is still predominantly an agricultural area and the garden's designer, Antonella Sartogo Daroda, a *paesaggista* or landscape designer based in Rome, has emphasized this by retaining and planting yet more olive trees. Providing shelter and marking the property's boundaries are existing carob trees (*Ceratonia siliqua*), and several groups of pine trees.

Because the ground falls away steeply, the strong colours of plants like *Hibiscus syriacus* 'Oiseau Bleu' and brilliant magenta bougainvilleas are silhouetted, dazzling against the sea. The part of the garden where they are planted is so high that the salt winds do not affect the plants.

The essential plants in the garden are not particularly known for their seaside qualities, but being typically Mediterranean they thrive on this site. Tree trunks and vine stems stand out in sharp relief against the white walls of each terrace room. In her plantings Antonella Daroda has added colour to the sober grey leaves and black trunks by close and dense plantings with bougainvilleas, *Lantana montevidensis* (syn *L. sellowiana*) and the strong pinks of

The swimming pool in the upper terrace is sheltered by a raised bed holding a frothy planting of *Lantana montevidensis* (syn. *L. sellowiana*). Pink bougainvillea stretches up from a lower terrace.

hybrid verbenas. Softer colour comes also from the Cape leadwort (*Plumbago auriculata*). The other essential plant in the garden is the oleander (*Nerium oleander*), a strong, drought-resistant evergreen shrub that flowers all summer long. Luxuriant masses of oleanders in scarlet, pink and white enclose some seating areas. Oleander is also used to underplant olives, providing a riot of bright flowers at ground level. The lower part of the garden is planted with lemons, grapefruits and kumquats in the Capri tradition, many of them in large terracotta pots.

Each terrace has a theme. Nearest the house, at the top of the site, are a jasmine garden, a rose garden surrounded by a vine-covered pergola, a white oleander garden and a garden of succulent plants where spiny spherical cacti and tall opuntias contrast with the dramatic angular shapes of aloes and agaves.

Just below the pool and house is the Bellevue terrace, furnished with olive trees and a semi-circular white bench. Here, the curve of a stone staircase between low white-rendered walls is emphasized by a swathe of magenta-bracted bougainvillea. Adjacent to this terrace is a children's playground and a swimming pool. Villa Anacapri is essentially a summer holiday home, so recreational areas are important. Further away, there is the Campo di Bocce, where a hard-surfaced sunken *allée* for playing bowls is shaded by large trees and overlooked by a wrought-iron gazebo planted with roses. Trees are needed here to provide shade from the summer sun, rather than shelter from winds.

A flight of shallow steps in the Capri style, and then a steeper flight edged with the evergreen sub-shrub *Felicia amelloides,* lead to another sheltered terrace, the Terrazzo del Cantino. This is surrounded by lemon trees growing out of a sea of the soft blue spikes and grey leaves of perovskia. Pergolas are hung with sweet-smelling jasmine and *Solanum wendlandii*. Both pervoskia and felicia, with its bright blue daisy flowers with yellow centres, are good coastal plants for warmer regions. On either side of this terrace the light grey of olive groves softens the impact of white walls and blue sea.

The colours of the sea and the sky in this part of Italy are among the garden's attractions. The seascape is lively with fishing and pleasure boats during the day and frequently at night. In the evening the Bellevue terrace is the perfect place to watch from as the sun sets, disappearing into the water. It is cooler here than in the village of Capri and the breeze that comes off the water provides relief at the height of summer. Strong contrasts between open and shady areas of the garden bring respite on walks through it. The overall effect is heightened by the heady perfumes of strongly scented flowers such as jasmine, rose and lemon, held within the walled enclosures of each level.

The garden of Villa Anacapri is large by comparison with most gardens on Capri, and the position overlooking the sea, with no houses to detract from the plants and the water, makes the garden seem even bigger and more isolated from the outside world. When you walk in the garden only birds break the silence.

LEFT The Bellevue terrace floats above a planting of mixed oleanders, bougainvillea and olives, and offers sweeping views across the Mediterranean.

BELOW The low-growing *Lantana montevidensis* (syn. *L. sellowiana*) is used throughout the garden as ground cover and as an accent plant.

OPEN TO THE SEA

DEVON, ENGLAND

High above Dawlish in south Devon, the clifftop garden at Highover conjures up the feeling of sea travel: there is a sense that it might just float out into the ocean. Wooden loungers at its perimeter add to the illusion that it could be a ship at anchor, seeming to roll with the motion of the water as you take in the view, straight out to sea and horizon.

The sea is in fact the focal point of the garden, the major protagonist. For its owners, garden designer Naila Green and photographer Ian Green, perhaps the most exciting thing about gardening by the sea is the brilliant clear light. As Naila explains, 'An expanse of sea reflects back so much more light and it is intense and clear.'

In her clifftop garden in Devon, Naila Green has planted a framework of sun-loving shrubs such as lavender (*Lavandula angustifolia*), the robust, upright-growing *Euphorbia characias* and the slow-growing dwarf, candelabra-like pine (*Pinus mugo*). Weaving through are vigorous self-seeding plants such as evening primrose (*Oenothera biennis*).

Naila is lyrical about the sea itself. 'I love it to look at. It is beautiful, endlessly fascinating and always changing, from season to season, day to day and even hour to hour as the day progresses. The position of the sun and clouds can affect it dramatically. This has a huge impact on the garden, not only creating an ever-changing backdrop, but also altering its moods and colours. The sea also has mood swings moving from calm, balmy and safe to dangerous, wild and exciting. I also love its sound which is always there and also always changing.'

Just 0.4 hectares/1 acre in size, the garden has an unusual shape, about 27 metres/90 feet deep but extending for some 400 metres/1300 feet along the cliff edge. There is nothing between it and an 18 metre/60 foot drop to the sea. Only a relatively small flat area around the house, approximately 30 metres/100 feet long by 13 metres/43 feet deep, is gardened. The rest of the plot is left to nature, and coastal plant species common to this part of South Devon are to be found here: these include gorse, holm oak (*Quercus ilex*), pines and, in spring, sheets of naturalized daffodils with evening primroses taking over from them in summer. In this natural-looking landscape seating areas have been set among the shrubby holm oaks.

The flourishing natural vegetation supports a richness of fauna as well as flora and within the garden there are several wildlife habitats which the Greens are loath to disturb. There are badger setts, kestrels, stoats, a diminishing number of rabbits, lizards, slow worms and large crickets as well as butterflies, moths, birds and moles.

As with many seaside gardens, the soil is poor and sandy and there are salt-laden winds. Highover faces southeast, so it gets some shelter from the prevailing southwesterly winds, but it does tend to suffer from the east winds that accompany gusty spring weather. The wind, pushed up from the sea below the cliff, is in fact felt more on the wooden decking which surrounds the house, like a ship's upper deck, than by the plants at the cliff edge. But whatever problems may be caused by the wind, Naila Green is not prepared to erect additional shelter belts or fences to filter it out because these would also mar the view. In fact when the Greens came to Highover there was a fence at the cliff edge, and one of the first things they did was to remove it. Now the open aspect of the garden offers the most dramatic view, making the sea simultaneously backdrop and leading player.

In addition Naila Green believes in working with the situation and so chooses plants that will thrive despite the inherent problems, without any need for changes in the environment. Salt tolerance is a must, as is low maintenance.

The narrow gravel paths between planted areas open out into a circular space to take the view out to sea. The soft grey foliage of lavender contrasts well with the spiky foliage of *Yucca gloriosa* 'Variegata'.

The garden resembles a meadow rather than a formally designed garden. Naila replaced the lawn with large planting areas divided and linked by straight gravel paths at right angles to each other. Now as plants are well established the straight edges are obscured; self-seeders in paths and planting areas provide a random effect and thyme and spiky rosettes of yucca are among those that have spread into the gravel. Focal points, such as the ring of handmade bricks that encircle the formal meeting place of the paths, lead easily to an inner circle of shells and then to a blue bench at the cliff edge, designed to help fainthearts feel safe while they pause to enjoy the vast canvas of the sea.

Good seaside shrubs, particularly those with the narrow grey, textured leaves that tolerate salt winds so well, such as ozothamnus, lavender, curry plant (*Helichrysum italicum*) and phlomis, are grown in close clumps, supporting and sheltering each other. *Ozothamnus rosmarinifolius* and its smaller relation *O. ledifolius* are evergreen shrubs that provide a great show of densely packed clusters of white flowers in summer. The multi-coloured green and grey spike leaves and upright shapes of phormium, crocosmia and yucca, combined with the silver sword-like leaves of *Astelia chathamica*, contrast pleasingly with the small foliage and rounder, mounded shapes of *Fatsia japonica*, lavender and euphorbia.

In the shelter created by the close planting of shrubs and perennials are plants that are less likely to enjoy the wind but revel in the mild coastal climate, such as ground-cover roses, agapanthus, alliums and tulbaghias. Elsewhere, tough Rugosa roses, including *Rosa* 'Fru Dagmar Hastrup' with bright pink single flowers and hips the size of small tomatoes, make a good first line of defence, filtering wind on these south Devon cliffs. Evening primroses, verbascums and red hot pokers give height and variety to the borders, and in many places have escaped from the garden to colonize the wilder areas. Here, on the sandy clifftop, where weather conditions are tough, vigorous self-seeders and spreaders reliably flourish. Narrow gravel paths wind between the planted areas.

Naila Green is known for her innovative garden design, yet here in her own garden she appears not to impose any preconceived design. Instead she rejoices in its openness, its exposure and its beautiful views, and garden design plays a secondary part. She finds out what works and goes with it, turning to advantage natural occurrences such as the vigour of self-seeding plants, which in a more formal garden would play havoc with design.

The garden is decorated with finds from the sea shore: there are black and orange buoys, shells, arrangement of crab backs, ropes and some fishing gear. Benches and tables are painted black and weathered, like old tarred fishing boats. Sturdy glazed chimney pots are filled with smooth pebbles or support a terracotta pan of thyme.

ABOVE Chimney pots add height and focal points at intervals in the garden and support terracotta pans. Some of the pans are filled with sedums or creeping thyme, while others are receptacles for beach finds including pebbles, shells and wood.

OPPOSITE Plants in this coastal garden, such as crocosmia, yucca and olearia, are chosen for their vigour and ability to thrive with as little maintenance as possible. They are closely planted, so that they support each other, weeds are suppressed and they provide protection from the wind for lower-growing plants.

A PLANT PARADISE

SYDNEY, AUSTRALIA

The garden at Gingie (an aboriginal word for waterhole) is in a cliffside, waterfront location at Darling Point on Sydney Harbour. It is a challenging situation, but also one that brings many benefits, not least in the form of the generous and ever-changing views across the harbour to the north shore.

Another advantage is the fact that the garden is protected from most of the strongly prevailing winds and the accompanying heavy salt associated with an open beachfront position. In winter the northeast wind does bear directly at the house and garden but usually only for short periods. In summer the rain-bearing southerly wind brings cooling relief. Rainfall in Sydney is usually a regime of heavy summer rains followed by a brief mild and dry winter. The ample, lake-like harbour also exerts a modifying influence on temperatures, which rarely drop below 15°C/60°F in winter. Consequently, over most of the year the garden is warm and humid, experiencing a hothouse microclimate, with summer temperatures hovering around 35°C/98°F. The humid warm-temperate growing conditions and coastal location are the main criteria that affect choice for the ornamental planting.

The original soil, a typically poor harbourside sand, has long since been replaced. Through years of cultivation since the house was built in the 1920s, the soil has been improved with a mix of organic fertilizer and compost into a high-quality moisture-retentive growing medium.

For garden owners Sancha and David Dickson, house and garden are central to their family's life, the setting for everyday family occasions as well as for special times including major birthdays, anniversaries and such like. Over the past decade Sydney garden designer Peter Nixon has encouraged the Dicksons to transform the garden into a sub-tropical plant paradise.

The full-on pleasure of its harbourside position is enhanced by a cantilevered, sandstone-paved terrace that appears to swing out, almost dizzyingly, from the house high above the garden. The terrace is like a magnet, drawing visitors out to see the spectacular view, which at this point is at its most expansive. It takes in the whole area from Double Bay on the southern side of the harbour to Bradley's Head on the north shore at Mosman. And it is not static. Depending on the weather it offers a varied canvas. Sometimes, on grey misty days it seems quite European, almost like a Canaletto painting. But mostly it fizzes with the highly saturated, sparkling, unmistakably bright colours of the Sydney Harbour scene, complete with sky, water and gliding yachts.

The cantilevered terrace at Gingie affords close-up views of Sydney Harbour and opens up stunning overhead glimpses of the various levels of the plant-packed garden.

ABOVE Among the plants that provide seasonal colour from showy flowers are dwarf hibiscus cultivars, cannas and *Leonotis leonuris*.

FAR LEFT Flowers play an important seasonal role in this multi-level garden, but foliage, such as that of palms and yuccas, provides the year-round colour and framework of the design.

BELOW LEFT Growing to about 4.5 metres/15 feet and clothing a terrace wall, *Zapoteca portoricensis* (syn. *Calliandra portoricensis*) or white powder puff is a warm temperate evergreen with good foliage and fragrant powder-puff flowers that open late in the day and through the night.

As you look down from the terrace, it might seem at first that all the intricacies of the garden below are evident, suggesting that the garden is a sort of 'open book'. That it is not so is the triumph of Peter Nixon's design. The design object was to entice the visitor into the garden by concealing its best features, some of which are just glimpsed when viewed from the terrace above, but for none of the intrigue to compete with the drama of the dominating harbour view. Plant height and shape are the twin devices he uses to tempt further exploration. Taller plantings that offer a bushy density at ground level, such as *Murraya paniculata*, are used as screens to hide flower and foliage treasures at a lower level.

Peter Nixon recalls that the garden when he first came to it was filled with 'inappropriate plants of cool-temperate deciduous and herbaceous origin'. Plants such as roses, azaleas and iris, lovely as they are in the right situation, are unsuited to the humid hothouse conditions of this cliffside garden and are maintenance-greedy. He has replaced them with garden plants that grow in warm-temperate coastal climates around the world, at roughly similar latitudes above and below the equator. Durability and tolerance of the prevailing conditions are the entry ticket; after that the most important qualities are foliage texture and colour contrast. Experience has shown Peter Nixon that many of the plants that offer good foliage, strong texture and shape, as well as good colour, come from within four plant families: *Lamiaceae*, *Acanthaceae*, *Apocynaceae* and *Rutaceae*. These are prominent among the families he concentrates on here, and the result is a year-round balance of foliage-rich, floral sub-tropical paradise, heavy with fragrance, where there is always something about to burst open.

There is one main path that zigzags through the garden levels down to the sea-wall, by way of steps and platforms from terrace to terrace. The return journey is made up a flight of steps on the northern side of the garden. The bonus on the ascent is pendulous flowers, in season, of *Dombeya burgessiae* 'Joseph Bateman', *Brugmansia suaveolens*, abutilons and *Iochroma grandiflorum* (syn. *I. warscewiczii*), all best viewed from underneath.

From house level to sea wall there is a total vertical change of around 15 metres/50 feet. The steps and paths are made from clay-baked pavers of brick-face dimension, while the retaining walls, all draped with evergreen climbers, are made of sandstone. The sandy colours of the hard surfaces connect to the sandstone surround of a pool which is right down in the water of the harbour. The overall garden space measures around 40 metres/130 feet wide by 15 metres/50 feet deep.

The garden area on the level immediately below the sandstone terrace holds a stylish parterre. Its geometry is introduced to make a connection to the rather heavily deliberate architecture of the house; it acts as a plant anchor, and like any parterre is best viewed from above. At this point the

Immediately below the cantilevered terrace is the most visible area of the garden, a small parterre outlined with small-leaved box. Past this section of the garden overhanging foliage conceals the lower levels of the garden, inviting further exploration.

house and terrace impose on the garden scene, while at lower levels it is the plants that dominate the sightlines.

The framework of the parterre is outlined with small-leaved box (*Buxus microphylla*). Black mondo grass (*Ophiopogon planiscapus* 'Nigrescens') alternating with stonecrop (*Sedum glauca*) fill the parterre compartments, with cones of small-leaved ivy (*Hedera helix*) at the centre of each square. The wall behind the parterre is covered by the lavish foliage and old-gold flowers of the giant Burmese honeysuckle (*Lonicera hildebrandiana*). The parterre planting is tied in at its northern edge with a hedge of the Florida fiddlewood (*Citharexylum fruticosum*), shaped to follow the line of the adjacent steps.

Lining the boundaries is a framework of evergreen shrubs including *Escallonia bifida,* which covers the southern end, and various natives such as *Syzygium paniculatum* and *S. australe* (lilly pilly) along the northern end.

Repeat plantings of orange jasmine, also known as jessamine or mock orange (*Murraya paniculata*), at around 3 metres/10 feet, and bush cherry (*Syzygium paniculatum*), shaped into a giant cone at around 5 metres/16 feet, among the plants he favoured. He added vegetable gardens and orchards, as well as a small farm.

In 1934, plagued by gambling debts, Courmes threw himself into the sea. His widow sold the property to aeroplane magnate Henry Potez, who lived there full-time during the Second World War. The garden saw its heyday under his care. He hired twenty gardeners and landscaped more and more terraces on which he planted hundreds of southern-hemisphere species. It was also Potez who built one of the garden's most striking features, a majestic, cypress-punctuated stone staircase.

Pelargoniums billow over the original balcony-like terraces of the former Riviera garden of Le Domaine du Rayol. Now redesigned to hold plants from Mediterranean regions from all around the world, Rayol is a protected coastal site.

ABOVE Terracing, forming balconies and decks on different levels, provides settings for dramatic plantings that frame the view over the sea's expanse. Bougainvillea and lantana follow the shape of the stairway near the original domestic buildings on the property.

ABOVE RIGHT The inflorescence of *Agave americana* towers above an area of succulents, including cacti and yuccas from Central America and the southern United States, and, in the foreground, *Agave attenuata*.

Later Potez used Le Domaine du Rayol as a second residence and although it was maintained to a certain degree, it entered into a lengthy period of decline. In the 1970s financial troubles forced him to sell it to an insurance company, which regarded it as a potential residential development site. In the late 1980s the local inhabitants formed an association which resulted in the acquisition of Le Domaine du Rayol by the state in the guise of the *Conservatoire de l'espace littoral et des rivages lacustres* (Conservatory of Coastal Areas and Lake Shores). This is an organization formed in 1975, inspired by the United Kingdom's National Trust. By the year 2000 it had acquired 423 sites totalling some 60,000 hectares/150,00 acres of land along the shorelines of France. All of its sites are open to the public.

When the Conservatoire acquired the now 19 hectare/47 acre estate of Le Domaine du Rayol in 1989, French landscape architect Gilles Clément was asked to redesign it. The estate had in effect been left to run wild over the previous fifteen years. Clément, inspired by the variety of different areas and landscapes on the site, decided to create a set of gardens or biomes that would reflect the landscapes and flora of the many regions around the world with

Mediterranean climates. These include the Mediterranean itself, southeastern California, central Chile, southern Australia and the Cape region of South Africa. Most of these Mediterranean climate areas are located between the same latitudes above and below the equator on the western side of continents and often are influenced by cold sea currents. They have mild and humid winters and hot and dry summers. The plants that grow there have adapted to survive summer drought. The aim of Clément's design is to take the visitor on a journey to other such landscapes. Many of the original plantings, including some that are non-Mediterranean – from China, Mexico and New Zealand – have been allowed to remain in place.

The gardens also hold interesting collections of plants that make up particular floras. The park-like garden is designed for walking through and learning about Mediterranean environments around the world. There are ten different areas covering the floras of the Canary Islands, California, South Africa, Australia, Asia, Tasmania and New Zealand, arid America, sub-tropical America and Chile, as well as a wild garden area. Ways through the garden are signed and thirty-three special plants are highlighted.

In the Canary Island area echiums flower in spring and the dragon tree (*Dracaena draco*) is among the representative flora. From Australia there are acacias, which bloom early in spring, eucalyptus, callistemon, melaleucas and Bidwill's araucaria (*Araucaria bidwillii*). From New Zealand there are cordylines and phormiums, which offer strong foliage effects.

The South African area features the fynbos flora of the Cape, which includes proteas, as well as some 150 species of aloe, massed plantings of Cape heathers and *Strelitzia nicolai*. Mexico's area boasts 300 species of agave, prickly pears, yuccas and dasylirions. Chilean puyas offer their sky-blue blooms in summer, while in late summer tropical plants such as bougainvillea and hibiscus flower. In late autumn the hillsides are dotted with strawberry trees (*Arbutus unedo*) in flower.

Clément introduced a management technique for the wild herbaceous areas of the gardens, as well as for the areas of different floras, which he calls '*jardin en mouvement*' or 'garden in perpetual motion'. The gardeners wait until the plants have seeded before cutting back in summer. This allows the natural dominance of certain plants to occur and it also helps prevent soil erosion, always problematic on sloping coastal sites such as this. The gardeners can control dominance to a certain extent as they can weed out seedlings that threaten to overtake other, more desirable, combinations. This management technique also results in a herbaceous meadow effect that changes from year to year.

The gardens are open daily except for the period between 24 November and 26 January when they are open by written appointment or telephone request. The seasonal beauty of Le Domaine du Rayol fascinated its first owners. Today it offers much, combining its former features with Clément's large-scale landscaping and generous planting schemes.

Cacti such as the peanut cactus (*Echinopsis chamaecereus*, syn. *Chamaecereus sylvestri*) grow well in the open, sunny hillside areas devoted to succulents. Like all succulents their foliage and stems have been modified. The stems are reservoirs of water, making it easy to survive coastal and other conditions.

A GARDEN RETREAT

CALIFORNIA, UNITED STATES

A passion for plants, clever use of found objects and a sloping site with views over a moody seascape provide the rhythm for a duet that landscape architects David and Isis Schwartz composed for the wooded hillside and modest weekend house that had once belonged to David Schwartz's parents. The house, sited on a rocky outcrop, overlooks Muir Beach in north California and faces east. When David and Isis came to live here – originally full-time, rather than just at weekends – the site was overshadowed by pine trees which obscured the dramatic views. Between them they transformed it into a garden to suit a range of age groups and filled it with plants that thrive in challenging conditions.

Many of the pines were cut down and the wood was used to support terraces and paths. Then the area near the house was levelled – there are now several decks, each affording shelter from a different wind. There is no prevailing wind but in the winter the weather can be so rough that salt foam comes off the ocean and covers the plants. The soil was basically clay and quantities of topsoil and soil improvers had to be imported before it was possible to grow any perennials or roses.

To accommodate their children, the Schwartzes created a lawn, play area and games area, as well as the densely planted slopes and terraces where they themselves could indulge their plant enthusiasms. All the garden areas are linked by wooden and stone steps, which weave through mounds of plants.

An attractive undulating or scalloped fence, the laths now faded to silver, echoes the waves and divides the land from a public right of way. The fence also prevents the children from going dangerously near a 9 metre/30 foot drop to the beach.

The garden is full of mementoes from friends and from work. As landscape architects, David and Isis are often able to salvage unwanted plants and wooden planks from projects they are working on and re-home them in their own garden. The scalloped fence was one such salvaged feature. Another, a stone with a deep hollow in it, now makes an attractive birdbath.

One flight of steps which leads to David's studio, also known as the 'Fish Shack', has a handrail of driftwood nailed simply to a driftwood newel post.Wooden laths are woven through the uprights to hold the design together. The Fish Shack with its attendant sweeping deck area makes another sheltered place to sit on or escape to. This is David Schwartz's bolthole, where

Mediterranean plants including the sky-blue spikes of *Echium candicans* (syn. *E. fastuosum*) and rock rose (*Cistus* sp.) combine well with New Zealand plants including *Phormium tenax* 'Variegatum' and the tea tree (*Leptospermum scoparium*).

SEASIDE EXOTIC

CUMBRIA, ENGLAND

'More Mediterranean than the Med' sums up the atmosphere of Charney Well, a steeply sloping garden that overlooks Morecambe Bay in Cumbria. It benefits from the benign influence of the Gulf Stream, affording owners Christopher Holliday and Richard Roberts the opportunity to create a dramatic garden in a style that garden designer Christopher calls 'seaside exotic'.

The mild climate, the openness of the situation, the bracing air and the constantly changing immense view of the tidal estuary of Morecambe Bay were the site's original attractions. Now, the hillside has metamorphosed into a garden surfer's paradise, as successive waves of billowing foliage of all shapes and sizes cascade and break on the slope. Plants with strong foliage and architectural shapes are the mainstay of Christopher's style. One group of plants in particular, New Zealand flax (*Phormium*) is a strong feature. Indeed one of the two British National Collections of *Phormium* is held here (the other is at Mount Stewart, in Northern Ireland). There are two species, *Phormium tenax* and *P. cookianum*. Where *P. tenax* grows wild in New Zealand it occurs as a coastal swamp or bog plant, while *P. cookianum* is a heath plant. Both thrive at Charney Well, where the rainfall is high but the soil well drained, and there is little danger of roots freezing for prolonged periods in winter. As well as dramatic shape, the various cultivars offer a wide variety of leaf colour. The strap-like leaves withstand most of the wind's battering and perform well in both sunshine and rain.

Christopher claims that the success of his garden is a happy accident, but his sense of drama and theatrical style, combined with the zeal of a plant convert, suggest that there is nothing accidental about it. The garden is by no means easy to maintain. For a start, it rises some 18 metres/60 feet from entrance gate to boundary wall. The slope is so steep that there is no possibility of using a wheelbarrow, as things would simply slide off; instead everything has to be transported up and down in bags, free-standing on a trolley. The weather presents difficulties too. On occasion the wind can be fierce, blowing plants as if coming straight from a giant hairdrier. And the area's annual rainfall of 1100 millimetres/43 inches can cause problems.

However, climate and terrain have conspired to provide many advantages which offset the challenges. Happily, even though the sea is only a quarter of a mile away, the winds are not salt-laden; moreover, the garden is protected from the prevailing north and west winds by the Hampsfell that lies behind it to the north and west. Much of the garden is on free-draining limestone, so rain is not nearly

Sunrise over Morecambe Bay brings the gleaming foliage of the upright Phormium tenax and the arching P. cookianum to life.

so much of a problem as it might have been. The overall pH of the soil is neutral, so it will support a wide range of plants. Best of all, because of its position on a tidal estuary, Charney Well enjoys mild seaside winters with temperatures rarely below –6°C/21°F, and cold snaps are few and far between. If there is snow, it is gone by midday. This means that Christopher can grow many exotic plants.

Mulching is one of the techniques he uses for insulation, to suppress weeds and, in places, to decorate the ground underneath plants such as yucca and grasses. He uses horticultural matting held in place with large pieces of driftwood and topped with bark, which looks as attractive as it is practical.

The whole property is just over 0.17 hectare/$^1/_3$ acre and is enclosed by stone walls to the north and west. Behind and some 4.5 metres/15 feet above the top garden is a mature woodland of broad-leaved trees and conifers (yew and pine). Walls and trees all help to moderate the wind, filtering it and creating pockets of warmth. The walls are suitable supports for luxuriant climbers including the evergreen *Clematis armandii* and the ornamental vine *Vitis coignetiae*. The tough seaside evergreen *Griselinia littoralis* has been planted along the south boundary, but this was done more for privacy than for protection. Christopher is careful not to place tall subjects in positions where they will block the views.

The garden is divided roughly into three areas. Up the slope and several flights of steps as you enter the garden there was once a heather garden. This, although low in maintenance requirements, was static in summer and no longer fitted with Christopher's planting ideas, which have evolved as he discovered the plants that suit his taste and the site. In the spring of 2000 he replanted the site, setting the new plants in a mulch of pea gravel over newspaper, which forms a barrier that slows down the merging of the mulch with the soil. Now the area, while still low-maintenance, is filled with exciting shapes and interesting foliage plants. *Yucca gloriosa* 'Variegata' and grasses such as *Stipa gigantea*, *S. arundinacea* and *S. tenuissima* and *Deschampsia cespitosa* predominate. Also thriving is the New Zealand toe-toe grass (*Cortaderia richardii*), a perfect tall grass for a coastal garden. The old stems never break in wind and can be left on until the new stems take over in summer. Alliums, including *Allium cristophii*, *A. schubertii* and *A. giganteum,* and eryngiums such as *Eryngium bourgatii*, *E. planum* and *E. giganteum* provide flowers, foliage and seedheads for months in summer and autumn. The plants combine well, all flowing together over the sloping rockery terrace.

The main area, level with the sunny-coloured house, faces south and east. The 'Morecambe Bay Riviera' terrace, with a slate surface, is level and has views straight out over the bay. Brute and machine force were necessary to create planting holes in the terrace, which was, according to Christopher, a boring flat expanse of slate. He used a pneumatic drill to make planting holes, lined the holes with compost and planted in dark-leaved cultivars of *Phormium tenax* Purpureum Group. Now their spiky foliage looks dramatic against the sky, the

OPPOSITE On a high point in the garden, bathed in sun, the essential seaside exotic style of this garden is most evident. Spiky yuccas, phormiums and *Cordyline australis* provide architectural shape and evergreen interest all through the seasons.

BELOW Grasses including *Stipa tenuissima* and yuccas such as *Yucca gloriosa* 'Variegata' are among plants growing in a low-maintenance gravelled area.

town below and the bay, especially at sunrise, when, silhouetted against the light, the leaves appear to filter the first rays of the sun.

In the garden areas near the house low-growing, mounding plants with softer, almost fluffy outlines, such as sages, santolina, osteospermum and artemisia, offer a pleasing counterpoint to the spiky foliage of phormiums – including *Phormium* 'Yellow Wave' – and cordylines. Here, too, several specimens of the palm *Chamaerops humilis* grow, unprotected, in terracotta pots across the front of the house, even in winter.

At the back of the house is an old boundary wall with a gate set in it. Once through the gate and up a few steps you reach the top of the garden. At this point the view shifts to the east and the garden, like a sunbather on the beach, seems to settle into an ample deck chair to soak up the sun. Christopher's planting is designed to take the eye eastwards, his intention being to obscure the roof of the house at this point.

In this more sheltered area at the highest point of the garden (which he describes as 'dished to the sun'), Christopher's seaside exotic style can be seen at its best. Here South African and Australasian specimens, including the ubiquitous phormiums, combine with other plants to offer a lush sub-tropical atmosphere. Height and luxuriant foliage growth is allowable here since it doesn't matter if plants obscure the view.

Eucryphia × nymansenis 'Nymansay', *Azara microphylla*, abutilons and the blue passion flower (*Passiflora caerulea*), which twines against the south wall, combine with corokias, abelias and Judas tree (*Cercis siliquastrum*). *Cordyline indivisa*, *Beschorneria yuccoides* and *Echium pininana* strut their stuff high above the house, together with palms such as *Trachycarpus fortunei* and *T. wagnerianus*, all of which benefit from the shelter of the walls to survive the winds.

Rock roses, including *Cistus × aguilarii* 'Maculatus' with large white, blotched flowers, *C. × purpureus* and the long-flowering *C. × pulverulentus* 'Sunset', *Aralia elata* and the yellow-flowered mimosa (*Acacia dealbata*), add to the sub-tropical cum Mediterranean style. The only plant that is trimmed back in this lush paradise is *Paulownia tomentosa*; Christopher stools it annually in spring to keep it at about 2 metres/6 feet and to encourage it to produce even larger leaves.

A particular benefit of the mild climate is that late-flowering plants do very well here. *Fuchsia* 'Mrs Popple', for example, often flowers until Christmas, while *Ceratostigma willmottianum* and penstemons flower well into autumn. Good doers such as these, and plants with strong and exciting foliage, provide an exuberant year-round framework for this seaside garden.

Planted into holes made in a slate terrace in front of the house, phormiums provide shelter and privacy and appear to filter the sun.

The relatively new garden (1995) of Mr and Mrs Robert Greenhill on Nantucket Island extends over about 16 hectares/40 acres and has 1.6 kilometres/1 mile of ocean frontage. The main house and its satellite buildings sit at the centre of the garden, high on a peninsula that juts out into the ocean. The natural way of things here is that plants are nipped and browned by salt-laden winds and parched in hot and sunny summers. There are also problems with deer, and to thrive plants must be able to tolerate sandy and acid soil.

Near the house, trees and shrubs that stand up to this climate, such as the Japanese black pine (*Pinus thunbergii*), the shad-bush (*Amelanchier canadensis*), *Magnolia virginiana* and some buddlejas, provide foliage and floral effects through the seasons. The impression is of trees and shrubs nestling close to the house for shelter. Trees are deliberately excluded from the outer perimeters of the garden: Oehme and van Sweden feel that lines of trees in the landscape would detract from the natural sweep of the bay and would make an ineffectual counterpoint to the horizontal, linear quality of the merging of sea and shoreline.

Around the buildings, planting is on a modest and yet intricate scale, with relatively small blocks of single species or cultivars, which gradually increase in size the further they spread away from the house into the landscape. Close to the house, the brilliant red *Crocosmia* 'Lucifer' grows up beside a glassed-in porch, looking striking against the wooden house, which has weathered to silver-grey. Sinuous paths, made from russet or blue brick or rectangular pavers separated by mown grass, snake from the main homestead to the various outbuildings, winding across the smooth green lawns. Each of the buildings is set in its own sea of softly swaying blocks of grasses, tall spikes of yellow verbascum and soft blue perovskia and swathes of eye-catching purple *Liatris spicata*. There is also a large unglazed porch or verandah where goatsbeard (*Aruncus dioicus*) provides a froth of white.

In contrast, Mr and Mrs Samuel Feldman's garden on Martha's Vineyard is older (created in the late 1980s) and, at 0.8 hectares/2 acres, much smaller. It is set back from the ocean but embraces the view across marshland and meadow to the sea. Near the house the simple lines of grasses are partnered by the more elaborate shapes and varied colours of native and non-native flowering perennials. As they move further away from the house the swathes of grasses and perennials swell in size, so that they lose their garden-plant characteristics and become more like the surrounding natural meadow. This apparently seamless transition from the designed landscape into the natural is helped by the use of a large proportion of native American plants in the garden itself.

To define the designed garden and make a border with the meadow there is a mown-grass perimeter path, which is invisible from the house. Here too trees

Plantings of perennials including *Achillea filipendulina*, *Persicaria amplexicaulis* and *Miscanthus sinensis* in the Martha's Vineyard garden are relatively tall and unimpeded by the wind.

are kept out of the plantings as these would detract from the wide vista over the landscape with its horizontal lines.

This garden is slightly less exposed than the Nantucket one, and the perennial plantings close to the house grow relatively tall and unhindered by wind. Here, near a grey wooden deck that thrusts boldly out into the plantings, a broad stripe of liatris contrasts in form and colour with brass-yellow *Coreopsis verticillata* 'Moonbeam'. Another strong yellow is that of the grey-leaved *Achillea filipendulina* with its dinner-plate-sized flat yellow flowerheads, making a strong contrast with the rust-red spikes of persicaria. There are large swathes of *Perovskia atriplicifolia*, lavender and well-established tall groups of eupatorium.

In both gardens there are native plants such as *Eupatorium purpureum* (Joe Pye weed), in particular the cultivar *Eupatorium purpureum* subsp. *maculatum* 'Gateway'.

The partners use many native plants in their designs, but they are not at all exclusive about it. Says James van Sweden, 'We use anything that works.' There is a special kind of drama and tension that non-native plants give to a planting. To achieve the bold effects they are renowned for, they frequently combine plants such as achillea and persicaria and design in huge masses, using numbers of plants of one species or the same cultivar. Plants native to North America which Oehme and van Sweden use regularly include liatris (also known as button snake root or gay feather) and coreopsis (or tick seed), and *Baccharis halimifolia* with its fluffy autumn flowerheads, a tough seaside plant that makes a good choice for Atlantic gardens. Also recommended is *Baccaharis patagonica* from South America: evergreen and more architectural in shape, it blooms in late spring; and the northern bayberry, *Myrica pensylvanica*. It is deciduous, resinous and acid-loving. In sheltered spots it can reach 3 metres/10 feet, but here it is always trimmed by the wind. The evergreen Californian bayberry (*M. californica*) is less hardy.

The signature plants of Oehme and van Sweden gardens are grasses, which are particularly effective in coastal situations. Blowing in the wind, they look especially beautiful and most important of all, they seem to cope well with salt. When the wind is very strong it just ruffles through the foliage and the plants bend and sway with it. The effect is almost liquid, as if the land and its plants had turned into water. Grasses also offer pleasing rustling sounds.

Miscanthus species from China and the many cultivars are heavily used, as are *Calamagrostis* species and cultivars. These contrast with the much finer panicums which Oehme and van Sweden also favour. The clump-forming switch grass (*Panicum virgatum* 'Cloud Nine') reaches 2.5 metres/8 feet and has glaucous blue leaves that turn dark gold in autumn. The plantings are kept very simple, and gently undulating clumps in large masses flow down to the shoreline.

Waves of colour are created using substantial numbers of plants. Here silvery blue *Perovskia atriplicifolia* rises from a base of liriope with *Lavandula angustifolia* in the foreground.

SKILLED
PLANTING

MARBELLA, SPAIN

The climate of the Costa del Sol on Spain's southern Mediterranean coast seduces many garden owners into thinking that they can grow a wide variety of plants. But, in reality, in the Marbella area plants have to be carefully chosen: they need to be able to tolerate not only high temperatures, drought and salty winds but also calcareous, harsh and badly drained soil. Christopher Masson, the designer of this Marbella garden, has been meticulous in restricting his plant palette to those that he knows really work in the prevailing conditions. It is this skill in plant selection that accounts for the garden's lush exuberance.

The villa faces south over the Mediterranean, with the garden descending by stages down to the sea. There is also a large garden to the north, much of it on the same level as the house. The view of the sea, enlivened by gleaming pleasure boats and picturesque fishing craft, is one of the joys of the property.

Some seaside gardeners can appreciate the sea in all its moods at a remove – especially if their garden is on a cliff or headland; however, food writer and kitchen garden consultant Susan Campbell, who gardens on the northwestern Solent, in southern England, has to deal with the ravages of sea and wind at close proximity.

Fierce southwesterly winds lash the trees, and the sea regularly inundates a large part of the garden. And things are getting worse each year. The spits of land, the mudbanks that created a lagoon effect beyond the pebble beach, have gradually disappeared and the waves hit the rudimentary sea-wall more violently with each autumn high tide. What was a gentle walk down a well-used path to the beach is now a climb first over the steeply raised step in the new sea-proof porch and then over a long pile of boulders that protect the garden's boundary.

In spite of this, Susan Campbell has created what is in effect, from spring to autumn, a small earthly paradise. Among her advantages when it comes to choosing plants is her keen sense of observation. Walking along the coast, in the woods and marshes she notices the plants that grow wild, then tries to find an improved horticultural variety that will thrive in the prevailing conditions.

Although proximity to the sea can cause havoc, the site nonetheless has distinct advantages. The view across the Solent to the Isle of Wight is beautiful. Herons flap lazily along a shore populated by busy oystercatchers, with their

The tamarisk is a tough sea-front survivor. Here it copes with fierce southwesterlies and inundation. On calmer days its frothy flowers mimic spindrift foaming in the waves.

ABOVE AND ABOVE RIGHT In the wilder areas reeds, hogweed and native grasses survive the wind and salt water, while the brackish pond is home to ducks.

OPPOSITE Near to the house, thriving in its shelter, is a collection of containers. Here the striking foliage of *Agave americanum*, *Aeonium* 'Zwartkop' and *Crassula ovata* are softened by pelargoniums. Shells and shards of china make a typical seaside mulch.

piping whistles, and a variety of geese and ducks; boats sail up and down and the ever-changing light gleams across the water, silvering the muddy spits or gilding the land opposite. Moreover, the garden was once agricultural land and so it has good soil, a rich loamy clay; there is a natural spring, too.

The Campbells have lived in the house since 1968 when their young sons enjoyed sailing and swimming, and for a long time Susan Campbell concentrated on growing vegetables. It is only in the last few years that she has turned to creating a pleasure garden.

A sheltering hedge of *Lycium chinense*, a shrub introduced from China in 1700 but now naturalized in parts of Britain, grows to the south of the house. On the south-facing wall of the house a Japanese quince (*Chaenomeles japonica*), fruiting within feet of the sea, is also seemingly unaffected by the salt-laden gales. Sloes, tamarisk, oak and crack willow (*Salix fragilis*) are among the other original inhabitants of the garden. Thrift (*Armeria maritima*), a natural seaside survivor, is colonizing the piles of chunky stone that form the sea defences, and pale yellow horned poppies (*Glaucium flavum*) straggle over them, wandering towards the sea from the landward side. A deck made of robust planks of wood, weathered to pale grey, is the perfect place to sit and enjoy all this.

ABOVE *Cupressus sempervirens*, a typical feature of Mediterranean hillside gardens, offer shape and frame views. Growing at their base are typical heat-loving plants such as lavender and pelargoniums.

LEFT Burnt-orange trumpets of *Disticis buccinatoria* vie with fragrant jasmine atop the balcony terrace. On the next level *Actinidia deliciosa* provides shade and cools the iron struts of a pergola.

A SCOTTISH COUNTRY GARDEN

WESTERN SCOTLAND

ABOVE The garden at An Cala is sheltered by a ridge of dramatic cliffs and a semi-circular shelter belt of sitka spruce and sycamore, a foil for the colourful cherry *Prunus* 'Kanzan' in its springtime beauty.

OPPOSITE Astilbes, dwarf rhododendrons and bergenias provide good foliage and shape before their flowers appear. In spring cherry and pear blossom dominate.

Its remote and inhospitable position on the Isle of Seil off the west coast of Argyll notwithstanding, Sheila Downie's garden at An Cala is a perfect example of the way coastal gardeners come to terms with terrain, weather and site. Colonel Arthur Murray (later Lord Elibank) established the original garden here in the 1930s for his wife, the actress Faith Celli. It has since matured at the hands of interior designer Sheila Downie into a garden that glows with colour and interest through the seasons, particularly in spring.

Sheila and Thomas Downie bought An Cala (the name means safe haven in Gaelic) sight unseen in the 1980s as a base while their careers kept them abroad. In recent years they have come to live and garden here permanently. The house, formerly a series of slate workers' cottages, with a distillery at one end, faces southwest with sweeping views, on clear days, to the islands of the Inner Hebrides – Scarba, Luing, Easdale, Mull and the Garvellachs – and beyond to the Atlantic. For Sheila Downie this borrowed seascape is the perfect boundary. The view from the top of the garden takes in the tended, manicured landscape, then the sea and then the scattered islands.

The horseshoe-shaped 2 hectare/5 acre garden nestles against a ridge with dramatic jagged cliffs behind it. The cliffs, together with a semi-circular shelter belt of Sitka spruce and sycamore planted in the 1930s, provide protection from buffeting salt-laden westerly gales off the sea. Nevertheless, what Sheila calls the 'tall poppies' of the herbaceous border – hollyhocks, delphiniums and foxtail lilies – are badly affected by the westerly gales.

In ancient times part of the beach, and until the 1930s open to the sea, the west side of the garden is now enclosed by a 4.5 metre/15 foot high grey brick

sea-wall. From the house the ground slopes down to the rocky shore, the pace of the descent slowed by terraces and hedged garden areas.

First and foremost on the original shopping list of the 1930s was topsoil. Fortunately, importing this was less difficult then than it might have been today. Tons of topsoil were brought in to the garden, arriving in the form of ballast in steamships that came here to take on board cargoes of slate quarried near by.

Even so, it was a huge undertaking transforming this wild piece of land into what is in effect a landscaped country garden. The tempering effects of the Gulf Stream which flows here means a climate that is relatively mild: frosts don't last, so cold snaps are short and sharp, and snow hereabouts is unusual. The soil is acid, which has also influenced the choice of plants: abutilons, camellias, rhododendrons, magnolias and azaleas are among the plants that lend colour and excitement to the garden in late winter and early spring.

Colonel Murray employed garden designer Thomas Mawson to landscape the site. His creation fits perfectly into the shape of the land, and he made use of all the natural features, including the waterfall and existing course of the burn (Distillery Burn) in his design. The sides of the stream are lined with water-

ABOVE The burn was dammed by Thomas Mawson to form a series of pools before it runs into the sea. In spring it is framed by brilliantly coloured azaleas and a weeping pear (*Pyrus salicifolia*).

OPPOSITE Mawson used existing natural features such as the jagged tooth-like outcrops to create different areas in the garden. Here weathered bedrock has become the foundation for a rock garden filled with azaleas, conifers, bulbs and euphorbias.

tolerating plants such as filipendula, astilbe, mimulus and lysichiton. A clump of *Rodgersia pinnata* 'Superba' makes a strong foliage block alongside the burn. Mawson used the burn's natural division higher up the slope to create two distinct waterways. One arm of it is dammed in a series of pools and flows out to sea. The other is constricted into a rill descending in stages before disappearing underground. Mawson also used the jagged pieces of bedrock that were scattered on the land as the basis of rockeries and terracing for the garden.

Sheila Downie acknowledges that the original plan is masterly, holding the garden, house and view together. She has not altered its basic structure but has changed some of the plantings, replanted some beds and added many trees. Many of the original plants chosen by Faith Celli still survive. The flowering cherry trees that provide so much colour in spring were all the rage in the 1930s when Faith Celli chose her plants. Today some of the originals survive but most were planted too close to the then-new sea-wall and to salt spray. *Prunus* 'Kanzan' still blooms well in spring, followed in late spring by *Prunus* 'Shôgetsu'. At ground level a carpet of bluebells spreads year on year. Sheila's aim is to create a pleasing picture, which, over time, she can enhance, adding and subtracting plants as she wishes.

Sheila has changed the rose plantings in the garden from formal 'rose-only' schemes to less formal, more floriferous borders. When replacing a number of unhealthy roses she discovered that roses bred in Denmark survive the salty conditions well. Among those she recommends is *Rosa* 'Karen Poulsen', numbers of which line twin borders leading out from the sun room towards a keyhole-shaped pool. Reflected in the pool's tranquil water is a graceful weeping pear (*Pyrus salicifolia*). The roses are interspersed with herbaceous perennials, while fragrant twists of sweet peas swirl around the frames of wooden obelisks and pyramids.

Among Sheila's strategies for dealing with the need for shelter and wind protection is a sort of plant neighbourliness. Hedges of escallonia and yew line the boundaries of the various terrace levels. In the shelter of escallonias she grows the evocative Mediterranean cistus, while in the lee of a beech hedge, the continuation of the garden's sea-wall, she grows Japanese anemones.

Known for their toughness in coastal conditions, here escallonia and gaultheria are regarded almost as weeds, as they ramp away. Both the green and the variegated forms of the evergreen seashore plant *Griselinia littoralis* are well established and the New Zealand daisy bush (*Olearia macrodonta*), pear and rhododendron grow in a dense shrubbery which filters the wind.

Like other coastal gardens An Cala depends on borrowed materials as well as its borrowed landscape to add to its seaside appeal. Here walls, terracing, patios and pools all feature material gleaned from the beach. In pastoral mode, Sheila has recently added wire sheep made by twentieth-century sculptor Rupert Till: a flock of these sheep now grazes in wilder areas of the garden.

OPPOSITE AND BELOW Many of the flowering cherries planted in the 1930s by the garden's first owner Faith Celli, such as *Prunus* 'Ojichin', continue to bloom well. On clear days the view from the house past 'Ojichin' sweeps across the harbour to the islands of the Inner Hebrides and beyond to the Atlantic.

ABOVE In and outside the house at Belvedere Island views are important and nowhere more so than in this small shower room. A ship's porthole frames the palms, bay and mountains.

RIGHT Since all topsoil had to be imported into the garden, the deck and hard landscaping predominate. Grasses and palms (including *Syagrus romanzoffiana,* syn. *Arecastrum romanzoffianum*), whose foliage contrasts well with the rounded boulders, are planted into raised pockets.

FRAMED SEA VIEWS

CALIFORNIA, UNITED STATES

Within easy commuting distance of San Francisco, yet surrounded by breathtaking land- and seascapes, this garden on Belvedere Island in Richardson Bay has been designed to be enjoyed as much from within the house as without. Slung low on a boulder-strewn shore, the house seems to be more waterborne than land-based, and the small garden areas won from the bay and the building are packed with stylish and practical plants.

The property faces northwest and the panoramic view from the front over the water of San Francisco Bay towards Mount Tamalpais is magnetic. Both view and climate have had a considerable effect on the design of this garden. The changeable weather of San Francisco Bay called for a garden that could also be enjoyed from the shelter of the house. The garden elements were specifically placed so that they could be either focal points, or frames for larger views, and both of these aspects are as effective from inside as they are when sitting outside among them.

Although offering astonishing views, in most coastal sites proximity to the sea, brings with it a number of disadvantages. Here they are evident in the form of salt-laden winds and mists, as well as poor soil. The soil of the property is 'bay mud' with a high salt content and bad drainage. Topsoil had to be imported and raised beds made so that plants could be assured of a good growing medium. Planting areas had to have sub-drainage as well. The winds come from the northwest, bringing summer fogs and some salt. Plants, therefore, are chosen for their salt tolerance. On the bay side the Mediterranean fan palm (*Chamaerops humilis*), the pygmy date palm (*Phoenix roebelenii*) and the queen palm (*Syagrus romanzoffiana*, syn. *Arecastrum romanzoffianum*), together with grasses such as *Miscanthus sinensis* 'Morning Light', *Helictotrichon sempervirens* and *Carex testacea*, and the New Zealand flax (*Phormium* 'Sea Jade') all flourish.

The small floating wooden dock on the bay enables the owners to reach the house by boat or ferry, as well as by road. The property is open on the water side, but sheltered on the land side by a tiny courtyard containing well-chosen plants including a tree fern (*Dicksonia antarctica*), an acer (*Acer palmatum*) and a Callery pear (*Pyrus calleryana*). A stone slab fountain of California chert, a flint-like rock with a crystalline quality, blocks out the hubbub of the road. The stylish wooden fences and gates which discreetly give the house and garden privacy are coloured a deep taupe. Bright green bamboos and grasses stand out against this subtle background and *Sutera cordata* – used here and in other places in the garden – makes a delightfully contrasting and dense ground cover. The front door is set back, along a path decorated with hanging paper lanterns and a lidded stone pot which add to the oriental effect created by the very restrained planting. This secluded area of the garden is very different from the other side, which is also designed for outdoor living, but with an open outlook over the sparkling waters of the bay.

The two spaces are linked by a smooth teak boardwalk that zigzags through a forest of ferns and bamboo and over a pebble-covered 'dry creek'. Here in this sheltered and shady position, the square bamboo (*Chimonobambusa quadrangularis*), the evergreen Confederate jasmine (*Trachelospermum jasminoides*) and ferns such as *Adiantum* spp. and *Polystichum* spp. grow. This narrow passageway leads past a small shower room which has a round ship's porthole as a window, giving a beautifully framed view across the bay towards Mount Tamalpais.

The teak deck outside the living room, sheltered by the house roof, is used for outdoor entertaining. In front of it is a paved area, edged with large round boulders and huge half-shells and softened with graceful feathery grass flowers, from which there is access to the jetty. The spick-and-span decking is fenced off by post and wire and some rope, which makes it look like the deck of a cruise ship. Life belts hung on the side of the low wooden house are both useful and decorative, increasing the effect that the deck is that of a moored liner. Thus decking – which began as a garden feature in America and has spread rapidly to climates where its use is less apt – is used here very appropriately.

Beyond the kitchen and dining room there is a small herb garden in a raised planter and a terrace which curves out towards the water. The terrace is paved with random pieces of smooth bluestone and edged with a balustrade of rounded boulders interplanted with grasses, profiled crisply against the water. Set among them there is a large bleached scallop shell. The shoreline, with its rust-coloured boulders, has been built up with extra pale stone blocks up to the deck and terrace.

As well as a circular spa or jacuzzi, set flush into the terrace to protect bathers from the wind, there is an in-ground fire-pit. The fire-pit is used as a barbecue but also to provide warmth at times when summer winds are accompanied by the distinctly chill-making fogs characteristic of this part of California. The pit and the spa are articulated by a paving pattern that warns that they are there without creating an obtrusive raised barrier.

This is very much a seaside garden, with artefacts like shells, driftwood sculpture and a whalebone fossil adding interest to the planting. Crushed oyster shell is used as a mulch in parts of the garden.

The property was a collaborative design by landscape architects David Schwartz and Teresa Kennedy, with interior designer Stephen Shubel of Steve Shubel Design and Steve Holt of Design Build Alliance. David Schwartz (his own garden is described on pages 42–5) loves Richardson Bay, where he was born and brought up, and he has succeeded in imprinting his feeling for the natural landscape on to the design he has created for this island garden.

RIGHT Palms, including Queen palm (*Syagrus romanzoffiana*, syn. *Arecastrum romanzoffianum*) and the pygmy date palm (*Phoenix roebelenii*), are suitable for fast landscape effects and grow well at the coast. Boulders and giant clam shells add to the atmosphere around the spa pool sunk well below wind level.

BELOW In a sheltered passage between two distinct areas of the garden the square bamboo (*Chimonobambusa quadrangularis*) and ferns thrive. The zigzag walkway is raised over a 'dry creek'.

BORDERS AND A CUTTING GARDEN

MAINE, UNITED STATES

Penelope and Nick Harris have created on the Maine coast a garden with two distinctive areas. The main garden at Smallidge Point faces south across Kilpatrick Harbour, a seemingly sleepy haven, with astonishingly blue water dotted with yachts, while the separate cutting garden in an old tennis court faces east. The main garden, with lush lawns and stately borders, slopes down to the rocky shore. Although the climate is benign in summer, in winter raging storms often toss some of the large barnacle-encrusted boulders on to the lawn. In such conditions the garden is blown about, but more usually it is unaffected by winds.

The original garden was designed by Howard Kneedler for Nick Harris's mother, and in recent years Penelope Harris has adapted it to her own enthusiams. The transformation of the former tennis court into a stunning, yet by its nature ephemeral cutting garden, is among her contributions. For her, cutting flowers from the rest of the garden is anathema; the cutting garden gives her the opportunity to enjoy flowers in the house as well as the garden.

The main garden is sheltered on one side by mature trees including spruce, cedars, silver birch and mountain ash, which were already established when the Harrises took over the garden. Under one of the trees, an old mill wheel is used to make a simple but sturdy water feature.

As a gardener, Penelope Harris appreciates the tempering effect of the sea. The cooling sea breezes in summer mean she can grow in her seaside garden in Maine plants that are grown in English flower borders. Fragrant lilies, stately delphiniums, poppies, astilbes, dahlias, astrantias and veronicas are among the plants that thrive in the closely planted borders, in an acid loam soil known locally as blueberry loam. Delphiniums thrive and are left in the ground to overwinter under a mulch, often augmented by thick snow, and they increase in magnificence each year. Dahlias however have to be lifted and dried off. Nicotianas are grown each year to fill gaps, as are salvias, which are treated as annuals.

To create the breathtaking cutting garden, which fills half of the former tennis court, and measures 13.5 metres/45 feet deep by 16.5 metres/55 feet along the sea front, soil had to be imported to the garden. A mixture of good topsoil plus seaweed and crushed shells, it mimics a well-drained natural coastal soil.

The attractive fence round the cutting garden appears to be a textbook example of the right way to filter wind and yet prevent additional turbulence. Painted a soft greyish turquoise, the fence contrasts strongly with the bright flowers and yet blends with the sea and sky. However, its *raison d'être* in this case is not shelter from wind: it is designed primarily to keep out marauding deer. It

ABOVE Spruce and cedars are among the mature trees that provide shelter for this harbourside garden. Hostas are well established in their shade.

OPPOSITE Lilies, delphiniums, roses, astilbes and other so-called English border plants do well in the shelter of mature trees, cooled by gentle sea breezes in summer.

dips to 2.75 metres/9 feet in front but is higher at the back. Gaps between the boards and larger openings offer enticing views of Kilpatrick cove, but have the more important function of allowing a free circulation of air, inviting breezes into what was once a roastingly hot tennis court.

The large openings are decorated from mid-August by sweet pea 'Curtains', grown at the sides of each 'window'. The raised beds within the enclosed area – in which herbs and vegetables are grown as well as flowers – are rectangular and triangular, linked by paths covered with crushed pink granite.

The garden looks very dramatic from the entrance with rows of Shirley poppies and lavender. At first, Penelope Harris used both catmint and lavender as foils to the brilliantly coloured poppies, as she was not sure that lavender would survive. In the first year, both were pruned to the ground in autumn and both died. The next year, however, when left unpruned over winter, both survived and flourished. However Penelope Harris decided to do without the catmint and so lavender remains as a foil to the bright poppy flowers, looking at its floral best from the end of June until the middle of August.

The poppies would naturally self-seed but Penelope Harris prefers to sow fresh seed each year. Also grown, mostly from seed, for cutting are foxgloves, delphiniums and some magnificent sunflowers. When the poppy flowers are spent, the plants become dishevelled and are removed. Then the cutting garden relies on the lavender for colour.

A large pot, a copy of an old Maine pot found in a garden near by, made of reinforced concrete, creates a bold centrepiece. It stays out all winter, unfazed by any sort of weather.

Penelope Harris's aim is to create a brightly coloured garden to compete with the yellow and white of the house façade and the verandah furnishings. These cheerful colours she hopes will be enjoyed from the sea by people sailing past on their boats, and will pay a compliment Kilpatrick Harbour, lively with yachts with colourful spinnakers.

OPPOSITE ABOVE A yellow swing chair and hanging baskets of annuals are the flags Penelope Harris flies to greet and compete with the bright sails and flags of passing yachts.

OPPOSITE BELOW Perennials such as *Achillea grandiflora*, astilbe and *Nepeta* × *faassenii* are augmented by annual plantings of poppies and nicotiana.

LEFT Penelope Harris has created a breathtakingly beautiful cutting garden in the former tennis court. Here she grows poppies including these Shirley poppies (*Papaver rhoeas* Shirley Group), foxgloves, lavender and sunflowers.

SEASIDE GARDEN FEATURES

Apart from the most obvious defining element of all, the sea, there are many other distinctive features that are characteristic of gardens at the coast. Some look as if they have arrived more or less spontaneously, blown on the wind or washed ashore by the sea. Such are the pieces of driftwood, the odd shell or two and perhaps a glass, cork or plastic float from a fisherman's net, arranged with guileless simplicity here and there within the garden. Others are more evidently deliberate introductions, used almost as theatrical props.

Just as you can style a house with furnishings and objects that give it a certain 'look', so the seaside gardener can create a distinctive seaside style, using a mixture of traditional landscaping materials and items that resonate with references to the garden's coastal position.

Most seaside gardens, by virtue of their location in reality and in our minds as the venues for timeless, sunny vacations, are relaxed and informal, so recycled objects seem to suit them well. Their location is often the source of such objects, as for seaside dwellers beachcombing is a way of life. The ocean calls you constantly, drawing you to its side. At any time, but particularly at low tide, there is nothing to surpass a walk at the water's edge, parallel to the horizon, watching the sun set or rise, looking into rock pools, and all the while, eyes glancing down, following the pattern on the sand that the waves make, checking the shoreline for driftwood, old sea shells, netting, rope, water-worn

glass, coloured bottles and perhaps other, not so romantic, bits and pieces that the tides toss ashore. Failing beachcombing, you can find such items at auctions and car boot sales, on skips, at architectural salvage yards or in antique shops.

Some coastal gardeners, of course, eschew the seaside vernacular, perhaps preferring a degree of cool Riviera elegance to what one might call 'end-of-the-pier' whimsy. While the coastal position dictates the overall plant content of their gardens, these gardeners would prefer not to elaborate the seaside theme within the garden's boundaries. And in some gardens, for example the plant-rich paradise of Gingie, on the harbourside in Sydney, Australia, the found items that add charm to an informal seaside garden would look out of place. Nevertheless, for those of us who 'love to be beside the seaside' there is something endearingly appropriate about the variety of materials, antiquities and flotsam and jetsam that inventive and creative coastal gardeners bring to the coastal garden party.

There are no rules about using found items other than those of taste and inclination. There is almost no limit to what you might find and use in the garden but, realistically, with salvaged items less tends to be more. The use of a few seaside objects sets the scene, adding emphasis and often humour, but will not detract from the overall look of the garden. Use too many, and the danger is that the scene will begin to look more like a junkyard than a garden.

In all gardens the strategic placement of seats for visitor and gardener alike provides welcome respite and the opportunity to enjoy a visual treat, whether plant, statuary or vista. Here on Martha's Vineyard, Massachusetts, the Adirondack chairs, arranged as a family council, have become a feature in their own right, especially when unoccupied, appearing to take the air and enjoy the sea view.

ABOVE Seaside gardeners use a wide range of materials to create effects that enhance and emphasize the coastal location of their gardens. Shells and – as here at Highover, Devon – up-ended bottles sunk into the ground are suitable alternatives to bricks or terracotta rope tiles for edging an area of gravel. They provide a light and informal definition.

OPPOSITE Tidal treasure in the hands of a dedicated seaside gardener takes on a different role. Uprooted in a flood and deposited on the shore, these two tree trunks have become an arched entrance to part of Susan Campbell's Hampshire garden. In addition they are used as one of several uprights that support a rose- and clematis-clad rope swag.

SURFACES

Gravel, sand and shingle occur naturally at coastal sites and are a fitting choice for the surfaces of paths and for mulching borders in seaside gardens. Remember, though, that in many parts of the world it is illegal to remove pebbles, sand or stones from beaches. In Britain it is against the sea-defences by-law to take these materials off the beach. Individuals always think that what they take will make no difference to what seems to be a limitless resource. But no resource is limitless, and removing pebbles or other environmental materials from the shore damages the whole maritime ecosystem, which in many places is fragile. It also wears away at the security of coastal defences, which are vital to seaside dwellers. Instead head for the local do-it-yourself outlet or builder's yard and purchase pebbles, sand, gravel, shingle or stones.

Gravel and shingle are 'go anywhere' materials in terms of adaptability to size and style of seaside garden. In small gardens where keeping the lawn looking good is a relatively intensive chore, it is worth considering removing the lawn entirely and laying the area with gravel. You won't have to store a lawnmower, keep it in good condition and rust-free, dispose of grass clippings or worry about finding a salt-tolerant species of grass. Gravel is a boon for covering small areas where it is difficult to grow plants, say under trees or close up to a wall. It is also attractive used simply as a decorative covering, say to create an impression of a dry river bed or a shoreline at the end of an informal water feature.

Gravel and shingle also set plants off well. Plants appear to stand out, their shapes more clearly defined when planted into a gravel-covered area. Grasses in particular seem to be more shapely effervescing out of a gravel surface than in a bare earth border. And gravel is useful as a mulch: in colder climates it acts as an extra blanketing layer in winter; in warmer climes, in summer, it helps to retain surface soil moisture.

Naila Green at Highover, Devon, replaced a lawn with generous-sized borders linked by swirling paths of gravel. Any self-sown seedlings are easy to remove from the gravel, as it prevents them getting sufficient roothold, and the maintenance level is much lower than that for mown paths. The gravel makes a pleasing sound underfoot, and looks wonderful as it dries after rain. At the meeting point of the paths she defines the gravel with concentric circles of handmade bricks and sea shells.

Bark chippings play a similar role to gravel in terms of mulching and covering path surfaces. At Bronte House, Sydney, where the rate of regeneration of brush and bush is fast, the resultant regular clearing means that there is a constant source of bark chippings – hence the carpet-like layers of bark on the property's cliffside paths.

In coastal Maine, pine needles and shredded bark with logs to mark steps or changes in level are a popular combination for paths and walkways, while

gardeners on the mid-Atlantic seaboard favour timber boardwalks. In each situation materials that are easily available add to the sense of local style.

In Auckland, New Zealand artist Diana Firth remembers her grandmother's love of shells and uses bags and bags of them, some whole, some crushed and more to be crushed when walked on (but not barefoot), as the surface material of the paths that wind through her deep and colourful flower borders. At Belvedere Island, California, crushed oyster shells are used as a mulch material in parts of the garden.

Other decorative natural materials that are useful for covering hard surfaces include green slate chippings, slate paddle stones, white spar gravel, white marble pebbles, stone chippings and slates. Water-worn glass makes a very attractive surface, but the chance of finding sufficient water-worn glass to cover a surface of any size is small. Instead you can substitute glass chippings, beads and marbles. Glass chippings are useful to lighten shaded areas, and in full sun offer glinting, dancing lights, mimicking sunlight dancing on water.

FENCES

Fences, employed primarily for filtering the wind and protecting establishing plants, are probably the hardest-working features of a seaside garden. They may not be as decorative or as interesting as a planted barrier; nor will they encourage or protect wildlife, as a living hedge will do. But whereas shelter belts and hedging (see page 134) take time to establish and themselves need protection when first planted, artificial barriers can be erected fairly quickly. Even the barest cover from a chain or post-and-wire fencing system will be beneficial in filtering and slowing the effects of the wind. Some materials may need little maintenance, although others will need regular preservative treatment.

Of course, fences also play other roles. They can establish privacy and may be necessary to keep animal pests, such as rabbits and deer, out and children in. At Muir Beach, California, the undulating wooden fence lining the boundary between the property and the public access area of the beach offers privacy to the garden and prevented the owner's children from tumbling down an uneven steep drop to the shore. The curved top of the fence, whose undulations were designed to mirror the waves, helps to camouflage it from the

FAR LEFT Some beachside finds take on a more permanent role in the garden. Here a wooden pelican, perched on top of a pier timber, announces the drive up to Fiona Brockhoff's garden at Karkalla, Victoria, Australia.

LEFT Objects found on the seashore can be used for practical and artistic purposes. They can be arranged and rearranged; room can be made for additions and, when they no longer please, they can easily be moved on. Here, in Susan Campbell's Hampshire garden, sea-washed bottles and driftwood have become the subject matter of a seaside 'still life'.

Many seaside gardens display a degree of humour and creativity, particularly in the use of found objectst. Much ornament is the idiosyncratic expression of a purely personal passion for collecting seaside or fishing objects, such as shells, glass, driftwood, netting, floats, bone or fossils, arranged by the owner, at random or for a particular effect. Coastal gardeners are renowned for the artistic uses they have found for the washed-up remains of trees, the water-rubbed pebbles and the cast-off shells of sea creatures. Derek Jarman's iconic garden at Dungeness, Kent, where tidal treasures in the shape of glass, metal, bone and wood combine with flowers in the shingle, is one such, but there are many other examples of the use of seaside finds.

In Hampshire, Susan Campbell created an archway from one area of her garden to another using two huge trees, root-side up, entwined. At Highover,

Devon, Naila Green arranges fishermen's floats and netting on a bench overlooking the sea.

At one of Britain's most famous coastal gardens, Tresco Abbey Gardens, in the Scilly Isles, this tendency can be seen on a grander scale than in domestic seaside gardens. Surveying the garden from one of its terraces is Neptune, a wooden head, coated with sand to resemble stone – the figurehead survivor of a nineteenth-century shipwreck.

Driftwood is probably the most satisfying of all beach found objects to use, since it changes constantly, depending on how you turn it or what you read into it. Some gardeners use pieces of driftwood nailed together to form decorative handrails in between fence posts on a deck. Secured on to shed doors or fixed to walls, driftwood becomes a trophy, its antler-like branches transforming an

The natural position for a timber deck is close to the house. Here in a garden on Martha's Vineyard, Massachusetts, designed by Oehme & Van Sweden Associates, the low-level deck provides a refuge on relatively 'high ground', as it curves out into a swirling, almost tidal, mass of plants.

ABOVE The wooden steps leading to David Schwartz's studio and fishing hut, the Fish Shack, at Muir Beach, California, have handsome driftwood newel posts and handrails, which combine well with seasoned wooden uprights. These different wooden elements, with their individual textures, are held together, visually and practically, by thin wooden strips or laths woven between the uprights and nailed lightly in place.

OPPOSITE The deck at Belvedere Island, California, offers level ground for outdoor entertaining, as well as access to the floating jetty and transport across the bay. The clean lines of the post-and-taut-wire fence provide a safe and unobtrusive boundary between garden deck and bayside jetty.

ordinary wooden shed into a baronial hall. Preserved by salt and bleached by the sun, driftwood takes on a magical, almost ghostly look, becoming more sculpture than debris. And even if you cannot get to a beach to find it for yourself, there are companies that offer driftwood for sale.

Then again, perhaps more than any other coastal material, sea shells evoke the sound of the sea, and all sorts of memories of childhood holidays, and they are naturally among the most collected shoreline objects. It is possible to collect shells from the shore but it is not legal to harvest shells from rocks or rock pools that still house the living sea creatures for which they are home and security.

Sea shells have many roles in the seaside vernacular. Sometimes they are placed sparingly almost as elements of a still-life tableau, on tables or here and there on the surface of containers. Sea shells can make an attractive edging for a bed. Scallop shells in particular provide a decorative alternative to terracotta rope edging (but take care when weeding near them, as their edges break or weather to a sharp finish).

In her garden at Highover, Devon, Naila Green uses shells as random motifs around the rim of a central feature, marking the meeting of several gravel paths. On the Solent, Susan Campbell combines shells, pieces of china, skulls and bones, pieces of iron and driftwood with plants in sinks and pots that snuggle close to the house walls. At Belvedere Island, California, a combination of artefacts, such as shells, driftwood and fossil whalebone, is used creatively within the planting schemes.

Coastal gardeners also commission artists to create sculptural effects for their gardens. Some artists work in the found materials of the seashore: for example, there are artists who work to commission to produce driftwood sculpture. The bones of sea creatures, like driftwood weathered into another state of being, are frequent shoreline finds also much used by seaside garden artists. Others work in the conventional media of the artist: ceramics, metal and stone.

Nancy Heckler's garden, Oyster Point on the west coast of America, benefits from many sculptural additions. Two locally based artists, George Little and David Lewis, have created a series of amazing ceramic entities, half plant and half marine creatures. Some of them hold water, much enjoyed by the garden's bird visitors. Another local artist, Sue Skelly, made panels of woven twig trellises, which Nancy has fixed to the ruddy-coloured clapboard of the house. They look as if they could support plants, but in fact they are there for themselves, as decorative objects.

At Karkalla, Victoria, Australia, there is a mix of commissioned work using natural materials and reclaimed items that have been transformed into sculptures. They offer intellectual and visual stimulation, in part because each in its own way is so separated from the purposes for which it was originally intended. For example, a bright channel marker, once valiantly indicating channels for sea traffic in the harbour, is now a tall focal point in the vegetable evergreen leaves that turn from red to greyish-green as they mature. Prominent stamens give the flowers their bottlebrush look. Useful as a hedge or specimen shrub. Grow it in well-drained soil in full sun.

Calluna Ericaceae
Calluna vulgaris (shrub)
Zones 4–7 H 60cm/2ft S 45cm/18in

Heather is a useful late-flowering plant for sandy soils. It grows to form a bush-like shrub. Its thin strappy leaves take on a range of colour and from midsummer to late autumn it produces bell-shaped flowers in white and pink to deep crimson. Grow it in well-drained soil in full sun. Shear over after flowering to remove spent flowers and to encourage new shoots.

Campsis Bignonaceae
Campsis radicans (climber)
Zones 5–9 H to 12m/40ft

Roof tops and walls are among the strongholds of the deciduous trumpet creeper or vine. Its trumpet-shaped, deep orange or red flowers provide strong colour from late summer through to early autumn. Grow it in fertile, well-drained soil in sun. Prune it back hard in spring.

Carissa Apocynaceae
Carissa macrocarpa (syn. *C. grandiflora*) (shrub)
Zones 9–11 H and S 3m/10ft

Natal plum is a vigorous shrub with shiny bright evergreen foliage, spines on its stems and fragrant white star-shaped flowers from spring through the summer. Its leathery foliage and compact shape make it a good choice for a sheltering barrier hedge. It tolerates salt-laden winds and drought, but is frost-tender. In autumn its sharp-tasting, but edible, oval-shaped fruits ripen to red. Grow it in well-drained soil in part-shade.

Carpobrotus Aizoaceae
Carpobrotus edulis (perennial)
Zones 9–11 H 15cm/6in S indefinite

The Hottentot fig is a typical dune- or sand-holding seaside plant. It is a frost-tender succulent and the liquid stored within its long fleshy triangular leaves is a useful antidote for jellyfish stings and sand

rashes. In spring and summer it produces yellow, pink or mauve daisy-like flowers that open in full sun; they are followed by edible, but unappealing, fig-like fruits in autumn. It scrambles over banks and if grown in terrace beds will overhang walls. It tolerates wind, salt and drought and in many areas where it has been introduced it is classified as invasive. Grow it in well-drained soil in full sun.

Caryopteris Verbenaceae
Caryopteris × *clandonensis* (shrub)
Zones 6–9 H and S 1m/3ft

Known variously as bluebeard or blue mist, caryopteris thrives in dry conditions, its silvery foliage helping to reduce evaporation. It produces clusters of blue flowers at stem tips in late summer and early autumn. Grow it in light, well-drained soil in full sun and trim it back hard in spring.

Cassinia Asteraceae/Compositae
Cassinia leptophylla subsp. *vauvilliersii* syn. *C. vauvilliersii* (shrub)
Zones 9–10 H 1.5m/5ft S 1.2m/4ft

Originating in New Zealand, cassinia has upright stems with silver down and dark evergreen leaves. These equip it for hot dry situations and it tolerates coastal conditions well. Its fist-like flowerheads of small daisy-like flowers appear from mid- to late summer. It makes a useful hedging plant. Grow it in well-drained soil in full sun.

Ceanothus Rhamnaceae
Ceanothus gloriosus (shrub)
Zones 8–10 H 30cm/1ft S 2m/6ft

This low-growing ceanothus is a useful ground-covering shrub in coastal gardens. Its distinctive dark evergreen leaves are a suitable foil for the haze of deep blue flower clusters it produces from mid- to late spring. Grow it in well-drained soil in full sun.

Ceanothus griseus var. *horizontalis* (shrub)
Zones 8–10 H 90cm/3ft S 3m/10ft

Also known as the Carmel creeper and originating in California, where it is used as a ground cover in many coastal gardens, this ceanothus has fragrant pale blue flowers in spring. Grow it in well-drained soil in full sun.

Ceanothus arboreus 'Trewithen Blue' (shrub)
Zones 8–10 H 6m/20ft S 8m/26ft

The shrubby, almost tree-like shape of this ceanothus and its wind-tolerant leathery green foliage make it a suitable choice for the coastal garden. It produces fragrant deep blue flowers in frothy clusters, mostly in late spring, but with a few appearing sporadically later in the year. Grow it in fertile, well-drained soil in full sun.

Centranthus Valerianaceae
Centranthus ruber (perennial)
Zones 5–9 H 1m/3ft S 60cm/2ft

Red valerian is a relaxed and opportunist self-seeding plant. It is well adapted to exposed windy sites. It produces heads of small, starry flowers in red, pink or white. To prevent self-seeding, cut back almost to the ground after flowering. Grow it in poor, well-drained, preferably limey, soil in sun.

Cerastium Caryophyllaceae
Cerastium tomentosum (perennial)
Zones 3–7 H 8cm/3in S indefinite

Known as snow-in-summer, cerastium is useful and attractive as a ground-covering plant for stabilizing banks and spreading through borders. Its small linear grey leaves reduce evaporation, helping it to tolerate exposure in windy sites. The small white flowers spread like snow on the ground from late spring through to summer. Once established it will take hold and will spread over a large area. Shear stems over after flowering. Grow it in well-drained soil in sun.

Chamaerops Arecaceae/Palmae
Chamaerops humilis (palm)
Zones 8–11 H 3m/10ft S 2m/6ft

The dwarf fan palm or European fan palm is a slow-growing evergreen palm that provides strong architectural shape in warm coastal gardens. Its bluish green foliage unfurls to make fringed fan shapes and when established it produces panicles of small yellow flowers in summer. Protect from strong winds to prevent damage to the ends of the leaves. Grow it in well-drained soil in full sun. It is half-hardy to tender, but in cold areas it can be grown in containers and given protection in winter.

Chasmanthium Poaceae/Gramineae
Chasmanthium latifolium syn. *Uniola latifolia*
(perennial grass)
Zones 5–9 H and S 1–1.5m/3–5ft

Known variously as sea oats, northern sea oats or spangle grass, *C. latifolium* grows well on poor soils and is useful for holding banks and on slopes. Its flattened seedheads dance in the wind in late summer, looking particularly effective when it is planted *en masse*. Grow it in moist but well-drained sandy soil in sun or shade. Cut back stems to ground level in spring.

Cichorium Asteraceae/Compositae
Cichorium intybus (perennial)
Zones 4–10 H 1.2m/4ft S 60cm/2ft

Chicory grows in clumps and is useful as a soil-holding plant. Its basal leaves make mounded rosettes and deep blue, white or pink daisy-like flowers rise up the stems at intervals. If left, the flowerheads will self-seed abundantly. Grow it in well-drained soil in full sun.

Cistus Cistaceae
Cistus ladanifer (shrub)
Zones 8–10 H and S 1m/3ft

Bright Mediterranean light and reflected heat from rocky terrain always come to mind when I see the mounded shape of the rock or sun rose. It flowers profusely in summer, producing ephemeral papery blooms usually with central markings on each petal. It is useful in coastal areas as its small sticky leaves weather sea winds well, but in cold areas or in prolonged periods of frost it suffers dieback. Grow it in light sandy well-drained soil in full sun.

Cistus × *purpureus* (shrub)
Zones 8–10 H and S 1m/3ft

This cistus grows to form a bushy rounded shrub. Its greyish-green evergreen leaves are well suited to tolerate salt winds and it is frost-hardy. It carries its mauve, papery flowers from spring through to midsummer. Grow it in light well-drained soil in full sun and cut out any dead wood in spring.

Colutea Papilionaceae/Leguminosae
Colutea arborescens (shrub)
Zones 5–10 H and S 3m/10ft

This vigorous rounded open shrub produces a mass of yellow pea-like flowers in summer followed by bladder-like seedpods in summer and autumn. Its foliage made up of pinnate leaflets helps it to withstand salt winds. Grow it in well-drained soil in sun.

Coprosma Rubiaceae
Coprosma × *kirkii* (shrub)
Zones 8–10 H 1m/3ft S 2m/6ft

This Australian evergreen ground-cover shrub with arching branches and narrow dark green leaves with rounded tips is low-growing when young but grows to form a mature dense shrub. In exposed sites it will be wind-pruned. It is half-hardy to frost-tender in cold climates. Female plants have insignificant flowers but, if there is a male plant nearby to pollinate, will produce berries in autumn. *C.* × *kirkii* 'Kirkii Variegata' has a spreading form. Its grey-green foliage has white margins and as it is a female it produces berries in autumn. *C. repens* has a mounding shape and withstands salty winds. There are also several variegated cultivars that contribute colour. Grow in well-drained soil in full sun.

Cordyline Agavaceae
Cordyline australis syn. *Dracaena australis*
(tree)
Zones 8–11 H 3m/10ft S 1m/ 3ft

Originating in New Zealand, the cordyline is a familiar shape in many seaside gardens. Commonly known as the cabbage tree, it is frost-tender in cold areas. Its lance-like leaves provide a fizz of excitement with their spiky architectural rosettes growing on tall stately stems. Mature, well-established plants flower with clusters of small, scented white flowers, followed by round white fruits in autumn. The variegated form *C. australis* 'Albertii' has green leaves with cream margins. Grow in fertile, well-drained soil in sun or shade.

Corokia Cornaceae
Corokia cotoneaster (shrub)
Zones 9-10 H 2.5m/8ft S 3m/10ft

Hailing from New Zealand, the wire-netting bush, which looks as if it has been blown in by the wind, is a wind-tolerant evergreen plant that suits coastal gardens. *C. cotoneaster* has wiry, brown stems, small glossy leaves and perfumed yellow blooms that are followed by red fruits. Grow it in fertile, well-drained soil in full sun.

Corokia buddlejoides (shrub)
Zones 9–10 H and S 3m/10ft

Glossy, almost leathery, narrow evergreen leaves, with grey undersides and on grey stems, make this corokia salt- and wind-tolerant. It responds well to pruning and can be used to make a useful light hedge. Its small yellow flowers are followed by red-black berries. Grow it in well-drained soil in full sun.

Corokia × *virgata* (shrub)
Zones 8–10 H and S 3m/10ft

Also from New Zealand, this evergreen corokia has an upright form. Its star-shaped yellow flowers are followed by orange fruits in autumn. It is wind-tolerant and can be used to shelter other plants. Grow it in fertile, well-drained soil in full sun.

Cortaderia Poaceae/Gramineae
Cortaderia selloana 'Sunningdale Silver'
(perennial grass)
Zones 7–10 H 2.5m/8ft S 2 m/6ft

Pampas grass is an elegant, clump-forming grass, with a strong architectural shape. Its erect, silver flower plumes blow in the wind, offering flowing movement. There are numerous cultivars, some lower-growing. Pampas grass is wind-tolerant and a substantial planting of it will provide shelter, especially if the flowerheads are left on over winter. *C. selloana* 'Aureolineata' will light up the garden with its golden-yellow foliage markings. Grow it in well-drained soil in sun. The old foliage should be removed in spring (some gardeners burn it out).

Cotoneaster Rosaceae
There are numerous deciduous and evergreen cotoneaster shrubs and trees, of varying heights, shapes and growth habits, that provide ornament (in the form of flowers, foliage and fruit), low-growing ground cover and filtering hedge cover in coastal gardens.

Cotoneaster lacteus (shrub)
Zones 7–11 H and S 4m/13ft

Known as the rock spray cotoneaster, probably because the frothy clusters of white flowers resemble sea foam. It has elegant arching stems, and the felted undersides of its emphatically veined

ACKNOWLEDGMENTS

This book grew from a seed sown by Barry Delves, one of the UK's leading gardening book buyers. My experience of gardening at the seaside in South Africa was the ground it fell on, and it has been nurtured to maturity by the generous natures of a number of people.

The garden owners, gardeners and garden designers who meet the daily challenges of gardening at the coast are the real stars. Mr and Mrs Robert Dudley-Cook (Lamorran House, Cornwall, England) and Mark Brent (head gardener, Lamorran House); Antonella Sartogo Daroda (designer of Villa Anacapri, Capri, Italy); Naila and Ian Green (Highover House, Devon, England); Peter Nixon, designer for Mr and Mrs David Dickson (Gingie, Sydney, Australia); Mr and Mrs Sandy Hanauer (Point of View, Long Island, USA) and designer Connie Cross (of Environmentals); Association du Domaine du Rayol (ADORA) and Gilles Clément, landscape architect (Le Domaine du Rayol, France); David and Isis Schwartz, designers of their own garden at Muir Beach and the garden on Belvedere Island, California, USA); Barry Beer (Infinity Garden, California, USA); Christopher Holliday and Richard Roberts (Charney Well, Cumbria, England); James van Sweden and Wolfgang Oehme of Oehme, Van Sweden and Associates, Inc., USA, designers for Mr and Mrs Samuel Feldman on Martha's Vineyard, and Mr and Mrs Robert Greenhill on Nantucket Island (both Massachusetts, USA); Christopher Masson, designer of Santa Margharita (Marbella, Spain); Susan Campbell (Hampshire, England); Leo Schofield (Bronte House, Sydney, Australia); Renée, Lady Iliffe and Bruno Goris-Ponce (Villa Roquebrune, South of France); Mrs Sheila Downie (An Cala, Argyll, Scotland), Fiona Brockhoff and David Swann (Karkalla, Victoria, Australia); Diana Firth and Mark Burns (Hauraki Gulf, Auckland, New Zealand); Penelope and Nick Harris (Smallidge Point, Maine, USA); Nancy and Terry Heckler (Oyster Point Garden, Washington State, USA), Ulf Nordfjell and Ingrid Thuresson (Norrviken, Sweden); Isobel Greene & Associates, designers of Carol Valentine's garden (Santa Barbara, California, USA) and the Jackson garden (Monterey, California); Ron Herman (San Leandro, California); Ken Ruzicka (Fire Island, New York); Vladimir Sitta (Sydney, New South Wales, Australia); Arthur Erickson (Silver Bow Farm, Puget Sound, Washington State, USA); and Liz Morrow, Waimarino, New Zealand.

Thanks to photographer Jerry Harpur, whose lens has captured the essential beauty and attraction of these stunning coastal gardens.

Particular thanks are due to my garden writer colleague and friend, 'the other Barbara' – Barbara Abbs. I would also like to thank the following for general research support: Liz Griffiths (Australia), Sally Williams of Garden Literature Press (USA), Peter Nixon (Australia), Judy Wolff (France), Fiona and Ian Vanderbeek (Australia), Clare Kneen (UK), Gisela Mirwis (UK), Glynn Percival (UK), Ken Cockshull (HRI International, UK), The Royal Horticultural Society's Lindley Library (UK), Sue Phillips (UK) and Trudi Harrison (UK).

At Frances Lincoln I would like to thank everyone who has been associated with this book, and in particular Jo Christian and Anne Fraser for their understanding and support, Becky Clarke for her inspired design and Anne Askwith for her skilled editing.

Horticultural consultant: Tony Lord
Indexer: Margot Levy

Designer: Becky Clarke